When Barry Soble heard I was writing about my energy work, he sent me this note. After witnessing and participating in the difference between Old Thinking and new possibilities, he wanted me to share this with my readers and Facebook friends:

Jeanne is grounded in magnetic, energetic, safe pathways.

She will softly access at least one hidden yearning in as little as five minutes. All you have to do is open your mind and she will gently materialize one of your treasured pieces lost within. She will coax a chocolate bit of happiness to wash over you. With some gentle guidance and occasional sweet fudge nudge, time with Jeanne will awaken your dormant desire, desperately wanting to be rejuvenated.

Let her lightly float about you while she tenderly shares her granite, resolute wisdom. It's transferable, I can swear to that.

Post-its my editor attached to the manuscript as our writing adventure unfolded.

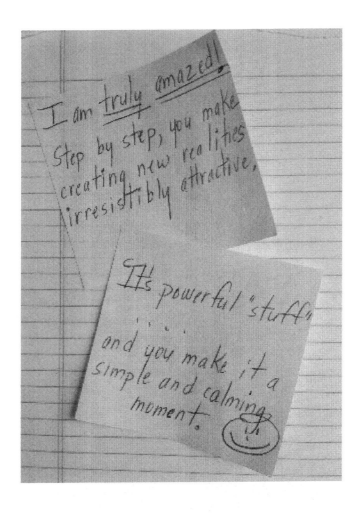

Words I Love

These are the words that pop up when my computer auto-corrects! I smile when I think about them tattooed like bracelets on my arm. Do any of them resonate with you?

Feelings
Wonder
Imagine
Empowered
Magic
Inner Wisdom
Possibilities
Dreams
Desires
Healing
Mystical
Chocolate
Personal Spirit
Embracing
Creating
Luminous
Inspiring
Treasures
Stories
Place of No Time
Path
Tickled
Potential
Self-Awareness
Curiosity
Friends
Love
Serendipity
Conundrum
Beyond
Change
Energy
Well-Being
Insights
Emotions
Ease and Joy

What's Inside

Old Change vs. Quantum Change / 1
Using the Guide / 2
Old Thinking / Quantum Thinking / 3
Notes About Energy / 4
Depend on Doubt / 5-6
Charlie and the Chocolate Factory / 7-8
Be Boldly Vulnerable / 9-10
Think Beyond Practical / 11-12
Allow Change / 13-14
The Secret Garden / 15-16
Forget About Maps and Itineraries / 17-18
Trust What You Know / 19-20
Float into Fearless Change - Guided Energy / 21-22
Conjure New Realities / 23-24
Reconsider Your Usual Days / 25-26
Create Your Reality / 27-28
A Check List for Making an Energy Shift / 29-30
Calvin and Hobbes / 31-32
Be Your Own Hero / 33-34
Penetrate Quantum Loops / 35-36
Break a Quantum Loop - Energy Dialogue / 37-38
Invite Energy Shifts / 39-40
How It Feels to Be in a Shift / 41-42
Ask for Energy Insights / 43-44
Liberate Your Perspective / 45-46
Winnie-the-Pooh / 47-48
Think About What You Are Learning / 49-50
Rethink Your Brain / 51-52
Notes About Quantum Reality / 53-54
Mentor Your Emotions / 55-56
Make Changes with Ease and Joy / 57-58
Provoke Your Promising Potential - Guided Energy / 59-60
Listen to Your Choir of Emotions / 61-62
Childhood Abuse and Energy / 63-64
Adore Your Truth / 65-66

Vanquish Stale Self-Perceptions - Guided Energy / 67-68
Feel It. Be It. / 69-70
Change Your Story / 71-72
Talk Forward - Energy Dialogue / 73-74
Seek Energy Messages / 75-76
Talk to Energy / 77-78
This, or That, or That? - Energy Dialogue / 79-80
Pull Intuition Out of the Mystical, Magical Realm / 81-82
Explore Why You Created Your Current Reality / 83-84
Pass Unwanted Energy Back - Energy Dialogue / 85-86
Follow Your Personal Spirit / 87-88
Expect Serendipity / 89-90
Uncover Clues in Conversations / 91-92
Tuning into Your Chatter - Energy Dialogue / 93-94
Repair Your Reactions / 95-96
Identify Your Tribes / 97-98
Transcend Blocks / 99-100
Listen to the Mustn'ts / 101-102
Slip Into a Place of No Time / 103-104
Look into Love's Kaleidoscope / 105-106
Be in Balance / 107-108
Fortify Changes with Creativity / 109-110
Where the Wild Things Are / 111-112
Acknowledge Energy Bubbles / 113-114
Adjust to Others / 115-116
Poke and Prod Labels / 117-118
Practice Placebo Healing / 119-120
How Energy Is Connected to Healing / 121-122
Bathe in Well-Being - Guided Energy / 123-124
Recruit Energy Buddies / 125-126
Work with Words / 127-128
Einstein Quotes / 129-130
Take Charge of Tangle Energy / 131-132
Smile / 133-134
Observe Your Change / 135-136
Where the Sidewalk Ends / 137-138
Nurture Your Dreams 139-140
Summon Your Haunting Dreams - Guided Energy / 141-142

Cinderella | *143-144*
Keep Going | *145-146*
Make Your Life Purpose Important | *147-148*
Gossip With Your Future Self - Guided Energy | *149-150*
Is Quantum Thinking For You? | *151-152*
Energy and Health and Well-Being | *153-154*
Energy and Healing Childhood Sexual Abuse | *155-156*
Energy and Codependence | *157-158*
Energy and the Power of Self-Awareness | *159-160*
Energy and Beauty | *161-162*
Energy and a Creative Path | *163-164*
Energy and Love | *165-166*
Energy and Menopause | *167-168*
Oh, The Places You'll Go | *169-170*
If You Like This Book... | *171*
Let's Connect! | *172*
Pondering Pages | *173-176*
Becoming an Author and Energy Healer | *177-178*
More Reading Adventures With Jeanne | *179-182*
Alice in Wonderland | *183-184*

Effortless to read and easy to pick up anytime, this book is for anyone who senses there's more and wants to explore their possibilities with ease and joy.

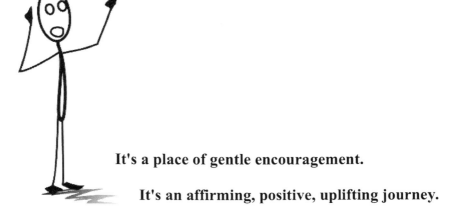

It's a place of gentle encouragement.

It's an affirming, positive, uplifting journey.

Reassuring, cathartic, calming, this book is a guide for people desiring positive change. It's life-altering, practical, and purpose-setting.

In writing this book, the energy field brought a stream of connections, too many to name, each one much appreciated and essential.

Then there were those who made this energy guide possible:

Compelling, exciting, crucial ~ *Linda McClellan* was the editor, an anchor of wisdom and insights.

Cherished and inspiring ~ *Chevy Kneisley* urged me to write this book and edited. Then she wrote the questions for the Pondering Pages at the back.

Nurturing, patient, always encouraging and celebrating my writing adventure ~ *Jim McElvaney* was my hero.

Incomparable, fun, and gentle ~ *Nat McElvaney* was my tech ally.

Appreciated, valued ~ *Kelsey Herold* and *Joel McElvaney* took me to my manuscript submission.

Truly intuitive ~ *Kieran McElvaney* took me a notch higher with ease and joy.

Delightful and imaginative ~ *Sherry Palmiter* translated my feelings into images.

Talented and generous ~ *Dimitris Christou* provided the perfect cover image.

Text copyright © 2016 Jeanne McElvaney
All Rights Reserved

Old Change vs. Quantum Change

If you're like me, you've spent considerable time trying to bring about changes in your life using the same old strategies. Maybe you've pushed forward using determination. You might have wondered why you didn't get what you wanted while others were making it happen. Perhaps, you used feeling-bad about yourself as your motivation. You might have started believing you don't have what it takes to complete what you start.

This book will show you another path to the changes you want in your life. It's a gentle, empowering, delight-filled journey. It's an unfolding that celebrates your spirit.

Instead of the tired, torn, and tattered map of Old Thinking, Quantum Thinking shows us that creating life-shifts is a flexible journey. It's more like making up your own recipe. In this guide, you will:

Find the basic ingredients you need to make the delicious life you desire.

Learn how each ingredient works to make the changes you want.

Be encouraged to season your personal experience in ways that are perfect for you.

Some of you will want a little more of one ingredient; others will omit ingredients. Each will mix the 64 ingredients of change differently, and everyone can create the personal transformation desired.

Along the way, you'll realize you don't have to struggle. You'll find that your good intentions are no longer fighting something deeper and stronger. Creating changes with Quantum Thinking means you are no longer the hard-working, overwhelmed Cinderella. You are the fairy godmother who makes it all happen.

> **"WE ARE MUCH MORE THAN WE THOUGHT WE WERE."**
>
> **JEAN HOUSTON**

This guide is going to give you 64 ingredients for making changes using energy. They are numbered so you can keep track of them not because they need to be experienced in any particular order.

You might like to use this guide as a daily reader and move through the book one ingredient at a time.

Or you might like to randomly open the book and trust that you will find the perfect ingredients for that moment in your journey of change.

Avoid feeling like these ingredients demand action; they are much more like dancing possibilities inviting you on an energy adventure. Get comfortable with the energy insight each one provides. Practice it. Invite yourself to be conscious of how the ingredient works as you go about your days.

However you choose to use this guide, you'll be most successful in creating a shift in your life by becoming a welcoming, gentle friend with each ingredient.

Einstein brought it to our attention. Now quantum physics is confirming everything is intelligent, constantly communicating energy... including your feelings, your thoughts, and your beliefs. And you can have conversations with that energy.

Quantum physics is showing us everything is vibrating, intelligent, connected energy.
That means we are part of a flowing ocean of energy. Our limitations are the rafts we create to help us feel secure.

Our thoughts, feelings, and beliefs are energy! Vibrating molecules of energy are constantly communicating with us in a dimension that has no distance.
You've probably experienced this when you 'knew' something about a loved one in another part of town or across the globe. With energy, miles don't exist. Information is instantaneous.

Energy exists outside linear time.
Though clocks help us coordinate our days, making changes with energy feels magical. The clock has no hands. Everything that ever was and ever will be is also happening right now.

We are only aware of 5% of what we believe, think, and feel.
The energy field can take us to information in the other 95%. We can discover what is powerfully affecting our choices and experiences but is beyond our awareness.

The energy field is vibrating, communicating intelligence. Science is finding we typically access about 7 bits of this information in our everyday thoughts and logic.
We can tap into about 40,000,000,000 (40 billion) bits of information when we are consciously using energy to make changes.

Imagine how remembering this information could change where you go to find uncommon answers as you create shifts in your life.

Old Thinking vs. Quantum Thinking

People and events create my experience vs.
I create my experience by what I'm thinking, feeling, believing

Energy and matter are different vs.
Energy and matter are the same

I respond and react to what exists vs.
I create my reality

The future is unknown vs.
I experience the energy I have sent forward

My five senses create my experience vs.
My inner world creates my experience

My possibilities are limited vs.
My possibilities are unlimited

The past repeats itself vs.
Anything we want exists as a possibility

What we can see or measure is real vs.
Everything is energy

What's visible creates change vs.
Consciousness creates change

Things happen by cause and effect vs.
Miracles are normal

#1

DEPEND ON DOUBT

UNCERTAINTY IS AN ALLY OF CHANGE. IT OPENS DOORS TO NEW POSSIBILITIES. IT INVITES NEW INSIGHTS.

Ambiguity is a friend in quantum change. When it comes to creating new realities, it gives us the possibilities of a blank sheet of paper with a plethora of paints rather than a paint-by-number set.

Doubt casts light into the the shadows of our life, illuminating new opportunities. In the chaos of our thoughts, we notice we're unsettled and what's getting too routine. Dreams from the past and new yearnings won't be ignored. We get uncomfortable enough to look for more.

The rumble of doubt can inspire us to release control and expand our life. It can show us that the way we have been managing relationships and circumstances is no longer working. It might point out a long-held belief that is no longer our personal truth. In the uncertainty of this feeling, freedom from outdated expectations often bubbles up.

Doubt can point out what we fear. Change often feels like we have to betray commitments or give up what we've worked so hard to create. Quantum Thinking reminds us that we get to choose what we include in our shifts, that nothing important gets left behind.

Getting a puppy launched a list of doubts for me. Was I ready for the change in my days, the commitment required, the unbelievably deep connection I knew I would feel? In the middle of writing a challenging novel, I was filled with uncertainties. Gathering information soothed my doubts. As I let go of old expectations, my husband and I discovered a different path for sharing days with a puppy. New information helped me release Old Thinking and my doubts.

Uncertainty is your heads-up to go to your inner wisdom for guidance. This is where you'll get clear, vibrant insights connected to the energy field. Turn away from well-intentioned advice, quiet your inner chatter, and ask yourself what you need to know… right now. A positive, empowering, and maybe improbable message will pop up. Trust it. It's for you. Keep asking until you *hear* your inner guide.

Doubt is the niggling energy that can empower change by making us aware of our inner wisdom.

"You should never, never doubt something that no one is sure of."

"Charlie and the Chocolate Factory"

by Roald Dahl

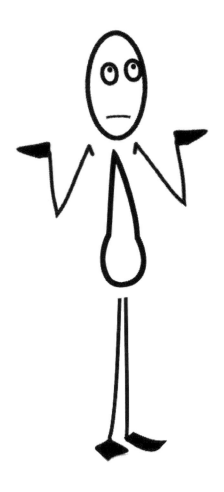

2

Be Boldly Vulnerable

Old Thinking has us believing we do best when we navigate the stream of life with a paddle and a plan. Quantum Thinking encourages us to release control so we can respond to the flow of possibilities.

We can't be our usual self and be in a quantum shift at the same time. When we are feeling vulnerable, we're experiencing energy that helps us loosen our hold on our current reality.

When we think of change, our fears bubble up. We think about what we'll lose and what we don't want to do. We're afraid we don't have what it will take. Often, our desire feels selfish, and we're sure we'll hurt people who are close to us. Quantum Thinking reminds us we will only experience these fears when they remain our primary focus. If, instead, we trust the process, we'll be part of a flexible, responsive energy flow that adjusts until we no longer feel vulnerable.

In the uncertainties of change, we are more able to feel steady if we realize we don't have to have all the answers before stepping forward. Our task isn't figuring out how. It's staying clearly focused on the shift we want so the energy field can respond. When I'm feeling vulnerable in a time of change, I often say to myself, "I only need to know what I want." With energy, the answers are found in the journey.

Practicing your new future helps you feel stronger and reinforces your desire. Start changing what you wear, so you can see your future-self. Spend an hour every day doing the very thing you want to experience in your someday. Rearrange your home in a way that makes your future visible. Practice is a fun way to empower your change. It also moves your emotions and thoughts, altering the energy pattern you are sending into the energy field to create your new reality.

When I began writing, I did it *when I had time*. Then I recognized I had unknowingly set limits on my desire, so I committed to writing for an hour every day. Now our guest bedroom is my writing retreat, mornings are writing time, and I take care of other things *when I have time*. **I practiced until I no longer felt uncomfortable in my energy shift.**

When you feel vulnerable, you can be sure you are allowing something new in your life. Boldly embrace this companion of change. It will help you release the need to control a journey that is empowered by open-minded flow.

3

Think Beyond Practical

Focusing on what we want doesn't create the changes we're seeking. It's more fun than that. We invite shifts in our life when we play with our thoughts, feelings, and beliefs.

"So do I focus really hard on what I want?"

That's what I'm often asked, and I'm so glad to say, "No. When you're making changes using energy, it's a lot more fun than that."

Every time we attempt to create a shift in our lives, we use old information to make assumptions about what we can have. This ingredient reminds us to soar with our imagination as we poke holes in old expectations.

Fly beyond what you believe is possible.
Right now, I'm trying to fly beyond my old beliefs about this book! I've written other books, and they have taught me that sales will feel like constantly dripping water. As I soar with my imagination, I want a different experience this time. So, when I walk my dog in the morning, I picture that trickle of water and see myself turning on the faucet. The handle turns easily. Books flow out of the tap and into the hands of people who are excited about learning how they can make changes in their lives using energy.

Float in currents of happy feelings.
My other books sales have felt like sitting under a shady tree on a summer afternoon. Pleasant. Appreciated. Quiet. For this book, I have a note on my computer that says **cartwheels**. Each time I sit down to write, I close my eyes for a minute of meditation. I imagine doing cartwheels across the summer grass, feeling joyful, free, and full of energy around the sales of this book.

Let new thoughts guide you.
In this book-writing energy adventure, I'm trying to catch old thoughts that are a fence around my potential book sales. When they pop up, and they do pop up with reliable frequency, I focus on the time I found a house to rent against all odds ... proving that anything is possible.

For shifts to happen, we need to nudge our feelings, thoughts, and beliefs in new directions. That's the challenge. That's the fun.

# 4

Allow Change

We have everything we need to make the change we want in our life. Energy "backpacks" hold untapped talents for learning curves, courage to forge new connections, and experiences to navigate uncharted landscapes.

It's oh-so-common and very understandable that most of us hesitate to sail into new waters. We want change as long as it doesn't change our lives.

Quantum Thinking assures us we get to tweak our energy shift each step of the way. It's a gentle experience, more like building a sand castle on the beach than catching a rushing wave on a surf board. We get to improve it with imagination, seeing what works as we go along.

Change is choosing to transform what no longer serves us. It acknowledges our biological inclination to expand. It doesn't ask us to give up the pieces of our lives we aren't ready to release. If you place a toddler in a small, safe yard with an abundance of lovely toys, she will explore with enthusiasm in effortless play. Then she becomes intrigued by what is beyond her current choices even while continuing to hold her teddy bear. She instinctively wants personal growth. Like her, we have a deep, inner need to expand our experience. The challenge is allowing it to happen.

Allowing change asks us to stop responding in the usual way. When our old beliefs, feelings, and thoughts become "backseat drivers" as we steer ourselves toward something new, they create chaos in the energy field. Mixed messages are sent forward, and we only stick one toe into the water of change. It's much like saying, "Yes, I want to go swimming" while shaking your head no and sitting down.

When I was opening my life to the wonder of writing, allowing it to happen was very challenging! I found myself avoiding the very thing I wanted. Even though I tried to make time for writing, I used that time to respond to emails and work in my garden. *Allowing* came when I recognized I was afraid of this change.

Allowing is on the other side of fear. Recognizing this is a first step. Then you can counter your inner chatter; *yes,* you are scared *and* you can still open your life to new wonder. Challenge your fear by visualizing yourself leaving your own play pen with teddy bear in hand.

In spite of your fears, seek change that awakens the magic in you. Then allow it.

"At first people refuse to believe that a strange new thing can be done,
then they begin to hope it can be done,
then they see it can be done,
then it is done and all the world wonders why it was not done centuries ago."

"The Secret Garden"

by Frances Hodgson Burnett

5

Forget About Maps and Itineraries

When making changes using energy, there is no best route. We can't follow the roads others have taken. It's a far more inspiring, intriguing, and insightful journey than either of these.

Manifesting quantum change is much like planning to go to Florida but discovering the reality we were seeking is exquisitely, thoroughly found as we pass through Georgia. Our destination is different than we imagined because we couldn't have planned all the intricacies that took us to the very best possible outcome.

In reality shifts, itineraries can be tossed and *thinking big* is a transcending ally. It helps us see beyond Old Thinking and worn expectations. It sends a message into the energy field that we intend to grow beyond *meat and potatoes*. We're ready to experience new tastes and anticipate the rich desserts in a full menu of possibilities. *Thinking big* invites more choices in our journey of change.

Using our senses as guides can ensure a quantum shift. It will happen more quickly if we repeatedly use our five senses to rehearse the change we desire. We might *see* the library through the eyes of our changed self, *smell* the laundry soap, *hear* our phone ring, *taste* our coffee, and *touch* our hair as though we're already in our new reality. These experiences link the change we want to the present moment, interrupting the energy connection that would give us more of the same.

When we trust quantum shifts, we open doors to our optimum path. It helps us see opportunities. It attaches to hope as we follow the winding, unfolding path of change. With Quantum Thinking, we recognize Old Thinking is holding us back. With trust, we can allow possibilities to carry us away, so we can see beyond our current reality.

You can't map your change, but there will be signs along the way. You may notice a certain topic, word, or idea keeps popping up in conversations, movies, or books. An animal that catches your attention could be a spirit guide. Mistakes, accidents, and physical symptoms can give us insights. Choosing to be open to the signs and trusting the messages they bring is both fun and empowering.

If you are reading this book, you're an explorer. Never doubt your discoveries in the energy field will change you.

6

Trust What You Know

When we choose to create shifts in our life, we step into a new landscape. With deep forests of old fears facing us, rivers of worries to cross, and mountains of doubt to climb, we have a powerful compass; it's our inner wisdom. It can take us on the most direct route to change.

You have a place inside you that holds your inner wisdom. It's your authentic self and embodies your personal spirit. This farsighted source of information is constantly communicating with the energy field. It always supports and encourages your life journey.

In your everyday life, you are only aware of 5% of what you think, believe, and feel. You make decisions with very little information, so habits and routines become your guides. You listen to others and feel social pressure. When you are making changes with energy, you seek your own insights and advice. You learn to trust what you know.

As you journey into change, you'll have many choices pop up. Like billboards along the highway, they'll offer you the usual as well as some unknown possibilities. This is your chance to create your unique experience. Close your eyes and focus on the choice. Ignore any chatter; the energy field rarely speaks in words. Stay focused on the choice until you see an image, notice meaningful colors, or experience a physical sensation. That is your inner wisdom talking.

Accept whatever comes to you. It will come quickly, feeling more like a butterfly landing lightly in your awareness than something as identifiable as a movie or photo. Like a new language, your inner wisdom has spoken its often unclear flash. Now you want to find words to express what came to you. This is essential, powerful, and often challenging. It's the step that brings your energy insight into your conscious experience.

As you describe what you saw or felt, you'll find there are more details than you first thought. You may notice your initial sense of color had a significant shape, size, or activity and is attached to an emotion. Or the strange lines you saw were sagging, soaring, or spinning. These are the kinds of descriptions that will come as you find your words. Although it may not be crystal clear, believe it. Connect it to what you were focusing on for the information you were seeking.

Finding your own, elusive answers with your inner wisdom is much like being given wings. It's always there to help you soar. The challenge is trusting what you know, finding words to translate your experience, and having the courage to act on it.

7

Guided Energy

With Guided Energy, you get to quiet your internal chatter, take a deep breath, and go on an inner world journey.

In this state of mind, you can release some of the anchors from your outer world to discover a new perspective.

You can gently visualize and empower the changes you want to make in your life.

You can also listen to this on YouTube.
Jeanne McElvaney Float into Fearless Change

Or use your smart phone QR Reader

Float into Fearless Change

Find a quiet moment when there will be no interruptions. Get comfortable. Take a deep breath and allow yourself to go to a place of no time.

Step onto a ship designed just for you. Notice its size. Its shape. Revel in its colors. Feel your feet firmly planted on the deck.

You are the captain of your ship sailing forward, feeling safe and comfortable. In the distance, you notice a sparkling, shining spot. It intrigues you and you move toward it.
Feeling excited and adventurous, you move into the sparkle.

You have sailed into the ocean of energy. No longer sailing across the water, you realize you can sail in joyous loops with no limitations.
There is no up and down.
You are in the quantum field of energy where everything is possible.

You are traveling where change vibrates. Invites. Encourages.

Without thinking about it, without attaching to what you already know, use the whispers of your inner wisdom and steer your ship toward the one change you want in your life that would make your spirit soar. Feel your ship sailing smoothly into the current that holds this possibility.

Notice the energy field respond to you like a gentle, warm breeze. Feel it enter your body, sending joy to every cell.
This is the change you want.
This is what it feels like. It's calling to you… a friendly, intriguing force that celebrates you.

Now see yourself standing on the bow of your ship, arms up in the air, a smile on your face, knowing you are ready to embrace the change you desire.

Bring your attention back to this page. Remember that creating changes using energy is a gentle journey of ease and joy.

8

Conjure New Realities

We have a natural, quantum ability to change our brain and body. Our magic wand is focused thoughts, not determination and will-power.

When we make a new idea more real than anything else, we initiate an energy shift. To manifest a new reality, we want to stay deeply connected to the vision until it feels more concrete than our old reality.

Our brain and body respond to what's holding our attention. Though our focus quite naturally falls on what we already know and creates more of the same, our imagination can give us new direction. Showing us a new and inviting path, it gives us an image so our thoughts, beliefs and feelings can realign and manifest change.

Creating a shift is like looking into a storm of 'the usual' and seeing a sunny new vision shining through. We feel the driving rain of what we've learned. We're buffeted by high winds of established beliefs. The chill of Old Thinking is hard to ignore. But if we *stand in the storm* and profoundly connect to the sensations and floating details of the change we desire... until it's more real than the storm... we are conjuring our new experience.

When we honor ourselves for doing the best we could every step of the way, we activate the change we desire. By acknowledging we've created our current reality, we can take the best parts into our new reality. What makes us feel safe, empowered, loved? Which beliefs, thoughts, and feelings are still serving us? Who will encourage our change by the way they live? How much wonderful can we accept?

When I was a divorced, single mom, my commitment to never marry again was strong. I had to grieve before I was ready to *stand in the storm* to create a new reality. Then I started walking to work and used that twenty minutes to refine, nurture, and embellish a new vision of marriage. When old thoughts tried to reassert themselves, I ignored them until a very different kind of marriage was more real to me than anything else. That's when I met my husband, who was a perfect fit.

You can set a new reality in motion. Find a daily, quiet moment to detach from your current experience, then use your imagination and feelings to attach fully to a sparkling reality you want. Float in blissful images until they become more real than what is in your life.

Like a magician, we can make new realities appear.

#9

RECONSIDER YOUR USUAL DAYS

FAMILIAR IS BOTH OUR FRIEND AND FOE. WE CAN LEAN INTO IT FOR COMFORT, BUT IT ALSO KEEPS US IN THE SAME PLACE.

Our routine days tease us into believing we are solidly planted in reality. Quantum Thinking helps us remember that there isn't "a reality". What we're experiencing is what we're focusing on while unlimited possibilities are appearing and disappearing all around us.

We invite a new reality when we're ready to live differently. It's like inviting a friend to come stay with us. Our routines are altered. We learn new things. We're more open. Along the way, we might sometimes wish things would go back to normal because change is edgy and familiar is soft. It's our desire to live our potential happiness that urges us to keep expanding our experience.

Avoiding change shelters us. It calms rather than excites. It doesn't poke us with questions or ask us to reflect. "Familiar" honors past choices that took care of our needs in our life journey. This still, deep pond of ease only bothers us when our personal spirit is ready for more.

If we continue feeling the same about ourselves, we'll create more of what we already know. Emotions lock our realities in place. To create change, we are asked to try on new experiences and review established beliefs, feelings, and thoughts. Moving out of what is familiar asks us to travel through a time of uncertainty.

When I was learning to market my first book, every resource advised having a Facebook presence. I resisted with excellent reasons; keeping life familiar was comfortable. But knowing resistance to change would stagnate the energy around my desire, I faced my avoidance and signed up. Learning and taking action soothed me during the transition until Facebook eventually became my new, familiar reality.

You empower changes when you routinely check in with yourself to see if familiar is defining what you think is possible. Dreams, desires, wants, and new intentions aren't comfortable buddies, but, oh, they make your spirit soar. And, as you create energy shifts, you'll be trading one kind of familiar for a different one.

The quantum field is a fluid and flowing experience. Sometimes we are served by grabbing a raft that feels familiar. Other times we'll want to swim toward new possibilities.

10

Create Your Reality

Quantum physics studies the nature of reality,
and we are wrapping our minds around
what scientists are discovering.
When it comes to understanding the stunning power we
have in creating our life experience, it feels like science
has donned a wizard's hat.

As we go about our days, it's life-changing to realize unlimited realities exist at all times. What we are experiencing in this moment is the result of what we believe, think, and feel.

Realizing we create our reality can feel unsettling! We're inclined to wonder why we would manifest the challenging parts of our life: a trying relationship, the plugged pipes, unfulfilled dreams, that sore hip. It's much easier to believe we have the power to shape our lives when we remember that we are unaware of 95% of the thoughts, feelings, and beliefs that are creating our experience.

We build our reality in the same way we build a house. Our beliefs are the foundation. Feelings are the structure. Our thoughts decorate. When we change any of these, the place we live shifts into a new reality.

Most often, everything remains about the same when we're in a shift. Like redecorating with a sofa, we mix the new with the familiar. But sometimes we want more; we want to remodel our lives. We do that by working with waves of possibilities in the ocean of energy where we live.

We are surrounded by infinite energy waves. Each of them holds the potential for a new reality. When we deeply, without any doubts, connect to a new thought, feeling, or belief, we alter our energy pattern. This flows into the ocean of energy and seeks a wave with the same pattern. When this link is made, the wave of potential converts into a new reality. We've manifested change.

Knowing this is life-changing. Nurturing. Even joyful. Although it's common knowledge that burgers and fries aren't good for our health, I consciously attached to a belief that connected my health to many happy memories connected with hamburger times. I hold my belief so deeply that I can feel well-being soaring through my body when I go to our local drive-in. I *know it serves me to be* sharing this joyful time with people close to me. That's my reality.

You are already unconsciously converting waves of possibilities into new realities. It happens every time you make a choice, take action, change your mind, or try something new.

"I GOT TO EXPLORE DIFFERENT WAYS OF GETTING ANSWERS TO QUESTIONS THAT COME UP."

ANJA

11

A Check List for Making an Energy Shift

1. Practice being in your new reality by 'feeling it', 'being it', talking about it, and writing about it.
2. Do <u>anything</u> that makes you feel good. Enthusiasm, joy, and excitement are the power emotions of shifts.
3. Take new action that is related to your shift.
4. Use positive body language and facial expressions that mirror your feelings about the shift you are creating.
5. Observe and release old beliefs.
6. Respond from your inner wisdom.
7. Remember old energy patterns are fading and new ones are emerging.
8. Remember repetition feeds the shift.
9. Think about the change you're seeking while feeling relaxed and focused.

> "IT'S NOT DENIAL.
> I'M JUST VERY SELECTIVE ABOUT
> THE REALITY I ACCEPT."
>
> "Calvin and Hobbes"
>
> by Bill Watterson

12

Be Your Own Hero

Past experiences create energy patterns that are solidly woven into the tapestry of our life. When we want to make changes, it's time to unravel threads that limit what we believe is possible.

In the energy field, there's no dimension of time. Everything that ever was is also right now. In this moment, we have empowering thoughts, feelings, and beliefs which are gifts from our life. We also have wounds holding us back.

Many people feel they can put the past behind them, but previous challenges stay with us. The emotional energy is part of who we are whether we are aware of it or not. It creates blocks, repeating cycles, and limitations.

Embrace your old wounds. You can be your own hero when you allow yourself to fully feel any discomfort around the change you are making. Rather than staying on the safe shores of avoidance, swim into the pond of sensations you usually dismiss. Invite the experience that caused your discomfort to join you. Explore what you have been pushing away. By acknowledging the pain, you invite insights that can release the wound so you can move forward.

Recognize your Magical Child. All of us have a child within who holds the blueprint of our core self. That child is who we would be if we weren't trying to fit into the world around us. He or she knows our potential and what we ache to share with others. No matter where life has taken us, our Magical Child is still holding this innate information.

You experience this wisdom when you do something that makes you smile when no one else is looking. In that moment, you are connected to your unique magic. When I wrote long letters while my childhood friends were playing tag or, later in my life, when my adult friends were shopping, I didn't know my Magical Child was nudging me. I became my own hero of change when I found the courage to share my writing. When you respond to your own Magical Child, it may not feel like a practical fit in your current days but, if there's something you do that makes you feel lighter and internally driven, follow your own nudge. Be your own hero.

Each time we choose to change, we view the possibility from a cocoon. Wrapped in what is familiar and comfortable, we are daring to imagine our butterfly-self. Be your own hero, emerge from the cocoon, and see yourself in all your beautiful colors.

13

Penetrate Quantum Loops

Quantum loops are repetitive, no-longer-wanted thoughts and responses. They feel like merry-go-rounds that will not allow us to get off and take charge of our life.

With 95% of our feelings, thoughts, and beliefs toiling away in our inner world without our awareness, most of our reactions are instinctive. Knowing more about an energy pattern, which I call Quantum Loops, can help us feel in charge.

Using association, a thought starts when our senses gather pieces of information and our mind connects them to previously collected impressions. A neural pattern is created. As our mind releases biochemical messages that bathe our body with the new data, feelings are generated and beliefs are set in motion. This constant flow is the underground stream that feeds the energy patterns of our reality.

Every thought has a biochemical brain reaction that communicates with our body. Our body responds, confirming the message has been received, and we feel relief when the message is familiar. You could even say, we become *addicted* to well-known exchanges. It serves us when we are urged to play a favorite song. On the other hand, it's an unwanted Quantum Loop when it means ignoring necessary paperwork.

Recognizing we're in a deeply rooted cycle can release the frustration of feeling stuck. It can help us understand why it feels normal and constant even when we don't want it! Then, we can turn to changing what has become a state of being, but isn't *who we are*.

When new thoughts replace usual thoughts, we break the flow between the brain and body. Fresh input leaves the old neural pattern languishing, and the biochemical wash is no longer activated; the Quantum Loop is broken. A new thought can be about anything as long as it consistently replaces the kind of thoughts feeding the Quantum Loop. When I recognized I was in a codependent relationship with a dear friend, I choose to change our dynamics by changing my thoughts. Every time I thought about her, I consciously chose to think about fabric art. I let colors, textures, and designs replace my usual reflections. When I broke through my own thinking, our relationship flourished in a more satisfying direction.

Quantum Loops feel like a tug-of-war between the change we want and what we keep experiencing. You can put muscle behind the shift you want by pulling in a gang of new thoughts.

14

An Energy Dialogue for you ~

I created Energy Dialogues because they invite active conversations with energy.
They provide new perspectives.

These dialogues never insist you take action. No guilt or 'shoulds' come with them. They come as encouraging allies to expand your possibilities.

These simple interactions with energy help you tap into the 95% of your feelings, thoughts, and beliefs that are beyond your awareness but continue to drive your choices. They are playful, making change an adventure with a new guiding voice.

Break a Quantum Loop

There are things we do, think, and feel that keep repeating old patterns in spite of our best intention to stop them. I call these Quantum Loops. This Energy Dialogue is a first step to help you learn how to break one of these energy cycles.

*Choose a thought that is repetitive but **not** emotionally charged, like "my friend is always late." Energetically speaking, this thought has become a rut; you naturally slip into it when thinking about your friend.*

To break this Quantum Loop, pick another thought that pleases you. It doesn't have to be related to your friend, it just needs to be something you enjoy thinking about: maybe recipes, knitting, hiking, gardening.

Imagine a path in front of you that leads into your future. Off to the right is the deep, energy rut connected to your friend. In this Dialogue, you're going to create a new path off to the left. Every time you think about your friend in any way, go quickly to the 'new thought' you've chosen. If it was gardening, you might focus on adding new plants, enjoying the colors, planning some pruning. The important thing is moving away from your rutted thought and enjoying new self-contemplation.

The more often you do this, the more quickly you will build a new energy path that connects joyful feelings to your friend. As this happens, the rutted path will become overgrown with lack of use. In the near future, you will instinctively go to your new thinking, and your Quantum Loop will be broken.

Though you didn't take action to change your friend, this energy experience tends to create shifts because new thinking elicits different responses from the energy field. When irritation or frustration move to light and joyful feelings, you can't predict the outcome, but you can anticipate a difference.

15

Invite Energy Shifts

New experiences will be limited if we use current feelings, thoughts, and beliefs to define what we want. It's like using a telescope to see our destination when there is a whole universe of possible places to land.

Old Thinking would have us believe that change is often uninvited; life throws things at us, and we respond. With Quantum Thinking, we can use change as a tool to take us to the life we want.

Daydreaming helps us break through old expectations. It's the bridge between Dorothy's Kansas and the city of Oz. Reverie can connect us to new desires that are the first step in creating an energy pattern for change. Feeling relaxed while emotionally attaching to what we want is our own yellow, brick road.

By not getting excited about what we want, we think we're *protecting* ourselves from disappointment. Throw that feeling out the window with Old Thinking! Nothing has more power to create change than to get wildly, wonderfully, deliriously turned on about our new intention. Pure, clear, vivid desire is a magnet for manifesting the events and people we need to have what we want.

Initiating an energy change isn't about creating a game plan. First, we connect to how we will feel when the shift is complete and let that feeling inspire our first response. One-by-one, we let inspiration and responses become the steps as we move forward. This invites us to learn along the way and adjust. It encourages emotions to guide. It acknowledges that, when it comes to the 'how', we are in partnership with the energy field.

When my energy work pointed me to a move back to my home town, I began visualizing the steps to get there. I pictured packing and imagined our house empty after I cleaned it. I focused on what I knew about this path and trusted the energy field to connect me to everything I needed for the transition.

Taking action is another way to advance change. If you've been dreaming about selling the jewelry you're making, check out your online options. If you'd like to share your yoga passion, offer a class to friends. If you love baking bread, review the rules for the local farmers market. If you've imagined watercoloring, buy paints or sign up for a class. Any action is perfect. It changes energy.

When we fully grasp that we create our reality, change becomes a gentle ally. That's the challenge. That's the fun.

> "I learned the 'language' of energy within feelings and sensations, and I learned to trust it and work with it. Now I know I can feel my way into solutions and trust my intuition instead of spending months trying to think my way out of some problem."
>
> Glory

16

How It Feels to Be in a Shift

1. Shifts will unfold in the way you feel it, not how you are imagining or planning or wishing.
2. We are tuning into our connection to the quantum field when we 'space out' and become unaware of our body, passing time, and what is around us.
3. Shifts happen when our thoughts, feelings, and beliefs about it are more real than anything we're experiencing.
4. We experience energy like a slide show, not a movie. The 'slide' we experience is what we're focusing on. Our shifts happen between the slides.
5. We get edgy and uncomfortable when the energy pattern is changing. There is a sense of being between what was and what we're creating. We can soothe this sensation by letting what we want fill our thoughts, feelings, and beliefs rather than trying to figure out how to make it happen.
6. We are in a shift when our inner world feels as real as our outer world.

17

Ask for Energy Insights

Everything is energy and all energy is interconnected.
By its very nature, it's our invisible, omniscient muse who
is constantly communicating.

When we listen to this empowering source, we tap into information that exists in a dimension beyond time and distance. Like Wendy with Peter Pan, we remember we can fly.

An energy insight is the message we get when we listen to the communication between the quantum field and our personal spirit. It has a direct line to the 95% of our feelings, thoughts, and beliefs that are beyond our awareness. This insight is the other side of the conversation when we talk to energy and listen.

In the energy field, everything is a frequency pattern of information. The insights we can get are unlimited. Atoms, the smallest particles of a substance that can exist by themselves, are 99.9999% energy. They are bundles of interconnected knowledge that can give us insights that are light years beyond logic.

Responses from the energy field are most often images, physical sensations, and formations of color. We can depend on a reply; the challenge and fun is learning to trust what comes to us in the silent communication. If we have cleared our inner chatter and set aside our need for a particular response, whatever comes to us *is* the insight.

When I wanted to know if an online book-marketing seminar would serve me, I went to my husband. He cleared his thoughts and held the energy of me taking the class. **I cleared all my thoughts and opened up to the energy he was receiving.** Taking the class brought an image of walking with a ball and chain wrapped around my ankle. He then focused on me skipping the class. I *saw* a robin hopping across the grass. With my husband's help, I had an insight. One choice felt restricting. The other felt freeing. I skipped the class.

What belief would block you from accepting an energy insight?
Trust whatever comes to you. It's an energy insight! With this new information, talk to your block as you would a child who is facing a new experience. Reassure your belief with what you're learning about Quantum Thinking: how it empowers and serves you. Give wings to your energy insights.

Energy insights never tell us what to do. They offer a different perspective. They inspire. They encourage our best lives.

18

Liberate Your Perspective

Our point of view gets corralled by our need to feel safe, empowered, and loved. Change thrives when we open the gates.

Old Thinking has us believing our view of the world is the result of what is happening around us. Fantastic freedom comes when we realize our perspective is nothing more than focused energy.

Accept something new happening. We interpret events through our well-worn paradigms, instinctively placing them into what we already know. Like Little Red Riding Hood seeing her grandmother rather than the wolf, we don't notice details that could give us empowering insights. When we make it a habit to look beyond our usual acceptance of things, we tap into a great force of change.

Ultimately, we choose how we perceive things. This is one of our innate powers, and we can call on this power to support an energy shift. If we feel there is something we can't do, we can consciously and repeatedly choose to connect to an opposing belief. We can look for proof that outweighs a truth that took root in the past and no longer feels like a fit. Doing this affects our thoughts and alters our feelings. It creates a new energy pattern that will connect us to change.

Relax into mistakes. They can only exist within our current perspective. In making energy changes, getting something *wrong* is an equally valuable energy insight as getting it *right*. Both guide our heart's desire.

When I was getting online attention for my book, *Time Slipping*, I agreed to be interviewed by another author who wanted to include my insights in his upcoming book. I was thrilled. I didn't realize I had made a mistake until I saw the quality of his work. **In that moment, I got to choose my perspective.** I could feel honored by his interest and glad for an experience that helped me be more discerning or berate myself for my error in judgment. I chose to see it as an empowering opportunity.

You empower change when you create visions that resonate with your personal world. Like your favorite soup, it has to have every ingredient that is perfect for you. Then your desire will align with your most authentic self. It will unlock your reservoir of talents.

Quantum Thinking affirms that our life experiences are shaped by what is <u>in us</u> rather than what is <u>outside us</u>. It celebrates our unrestricted capacity to adjust our perceptions to create change.

"Hello, Rabbit," he said, "is that you?"

"Let's pretend it isn't," said Rabbit, "and see what happens."

"Winnie-the-Pooh"

by A.A. Milne

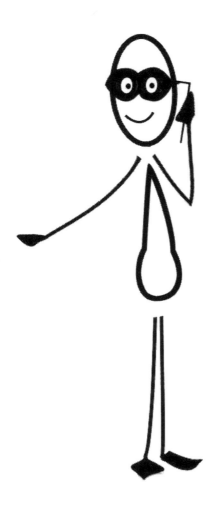

19

Think About What You Are Learning

We often feel that inviting change is like planning a picnic without a weather forecast. In spite of every effort, anything could happen! Using energy to create a shift allows us to forecast how our new reality will feel.

Once we step on the path of change, we are on a learning curve. That's part of the journey. That's the challenge. That's the fun.

You can't arrive at a pleasing change by struggling to get there. How you feel on the journey is defining your future feelings. I have a friend who has shared many adventures of personal growth with me. Our conversations bubble with excitement about possible ways to reach what each of us wants. As we make choices, he is the one who consistently asks, "What will we be learning about the change we are creating?"

Each step we take is teaching us something about how we will feel when our wish becomes our new reality. If I choose to sell my books by public speaking around the country, and I don't want to leave my husband and dog behind, I am teaching myself that selling books is a lonely experience. On the other hand, if I choose to sell my books as part of the energy sessions I offer, I am teaching myself that selling my books is joyous and offers me a chance to meet other people interested in making changes with energy!

As you create change, open yourself to all possibilities. Then ask yourself what you'll be learning with each choice. What it teaches you will become part of what you're creating. Daydream and imagine yourself experiencing what you want as though it's already happened. Notice all the empowering, good feelings you expect. Use these as your guide when you're considering your choices.

Ask yourself, what am I learning if I do this? Or if I do that? This question will be your compass for finding what you are seeking in a way that beautifully fits what is important to you. The future you're shaping will be more abundant if you pay attention to the foundation of feelings you're learning along the way. Every choice you make is teaching you how you're going to feel in your future experience.

The textures and colors of your future experience are woven with the choices you make along the way. Weave your journey of change with experiences that give you lessons that feel good.

20
Rethink Your Brain

Old Thinking encouraged us to make our brain "the benevolent king of reasonable choices". It's less than that... and more.

At any given time, we have access to 7 bits of logical information. The quantum field gives us access to 40 billion bits of information.

Our brain compiles life experiences to confirm what we know. New information automatically fires associated neural circuits to help us create more of the same. If we're seeking change, we're better served by *feeling about it* rather than *thinking about it*.

Though our brain is a network of unconscious responses, it can be changed by new thoughts. Like an eager student, the brain takes notes when we actively tweak what we are thinking, and it responds. We're the teacher choosing the content of our mind.

Both experiences and imagination have equal influence in altering our brain's responses. The brain doesn't know the difference between a deeply held, clear vision and something that is happening in our external world. In this, our brain is a profound ally of change. In our mind's eye, we can practice the change we want, creating a new energy pattern for the shift we're manifesting.

I agree that the only constant in life is change, and I love exploring my possibilities. Having a different relationship with my brain has helped me. I now know it's not a general in charge of my life, but I can use the abundant information my brain stores to make new thoughts feel so real, they become my reality. I can call on its amazing capacity to collect and associate everything coming in through my five senses so I can keep growing.

Rather than going to your mind for advice, work with it to generate an image that will be translated into your reality. Feed your brain new information using vivid images wrapped with supportive feelings, beliefs, and thoughts. Recognize your brain is always altered by fresh data that can create quantum shifts.

Our brain doesn't guide us. Instead, it aligns our inner and outer worlds, and this energetic connection is the source of our responses.

"What you do that no one else I have ever known does is present opportunities for participants to physically experience and interact with energy using the 95% of themselves that is unaware of their feelings and thoughts and needs."

Chevy

21

Notes About Quantum Reality

1. A quantum is a small pocket of energy.
2. Everything is energy.
3. Energy is intelligent and constantly communicating.
4. All energy is interacting.
5. We affect everything that has our focus.
6. We live in constantly shifting possibilities.
7. Energy responds to our thoughts.
8. When we can imagine something, it exists as a wave of potential that can lower its frequency pattern until it becomes solid and a new reality.
9. Matter constantly disappears and appears; it moves from a wave of possibility to matter only when we 'observe' it.
10. A 'quanta' is 10-30 million times smaller than an atom. At that level, consciousness determines its vibration, determining if it remains a wave of potential or a physical experience.

22

Mentor Your Emotions

When it comes to our feelings, we aren't minions of outside forces. We're the masters.

Emotions can paint our world with old expectations or bright, new possibilities.

Our feelings are the end product to everything we experience. They become a blueprint for our instinctive responses when similar moments arise in the future. Quantum Thinking helps us remember that we create our experience. That means we can change the blueprint and change the feelings behind our reactions.

Our emotions anchor us to our past when we keep recycling them. This emotional grounding often serves us. Just as often, the anchor keeps us from moving forward. When we recognize this, we are being invited to explore the source of feelings. Then we can consciously replace old feelings with current, empowering emotions.

If we persistently stay with the same emotions, we can't use new experiences to gather insights for nurturing change. With old feelings, we interpret fresh circumstances with stale steadiness. We lose the opportunity to learn lessons that could expand our awareness. When an emotion feels like repeating lyrics, we can choose to listen to new music and find something that feeds a new sense of ourselves.

I recently recognized I was bringing shame to my work. While friends cheered for me and others celebrated what I shared, I was looking through an old lens of embarrassment. I found the root of this limiting emotion in a childhood moment when I was accused of wanting attention. To change this feeling and redirect my life, I am saying to myself "I am safe to shine." I know that this mantra and finding the root of my feeling will erase my shame.

Your deeply held emotions are attracting more of the same. This energy is so strong, the Heartmath Institute has confirmed your emotions can change the shape of your DNA. To become a master rather than a minion, identify your limiting feelings, put them under a microscope of your personal truth, and see if they need to change.

In the quantum field, emotions are movement of energy. They are messengers between our experiences and our inner world. Created by our thoughts and beliefs, they are energies that can be sifted, shifted, and changed with intention.

23

Make Changes with Ease and Joy

In the energy field, there are a million paths to anything you want. One of them takes you to change with ease and joy. It's the one a little to the left, or to the right, of your usual path.

We've all learned to work hard for what we want; it's a solid belief in Old Thinking. Quantum Thinking has opened a new door to understanding how we create our reality. We get to choose the path we travel to change.

In my Old Thinking, I urged my children to reach for their goals using outlined steps, setting deadlines, knowing their destination. I was convinced that a good map would take them where they wanted to go. But **fortunately, I had a son who didn't listen**. He knew how his intention would *feel* rather than how it would *look*. Letting his days gently unfold, he took action as it felt right. He wasn't afraid to mix in a good amount of relaxation, play, and many directions of exploration. I loved how he manifested change, his way. His path scrambled my beliefs; I had my first glimpse of making changes with Quantum Thinking.

New goals begin as wishes. Translating these fluffy, feel-good desires asks us to step onto a new path. I've consciously chosen many different kinds of paths in my adventure with changes. The route that feels most responsive and powerful for me is a path of ease and joy. In everything I do, whatever change I invite, I say, "With ease and joy." I know I get to experience life shifts under this umbrella because the energy field always responds to what I think, feel, and believe.

You get to find your own empowering, reassuring mantra to guide you forward. When wishes, dreams, and desires tickle you, embrace them. Know you get to travel toward them in a way that feels right for you. In the moment you translate a wish into a new reality, choose how that path will feel. I have a friend who uses "peace and joy" Another keeps reminding herself, "no drama". You might like "with abundance in every moment" or "in health and well-being". I've always liked "honoring my personal spirit". Maybe "with heart and clarity" feels right. "Trusting my personal growth" made big changes in my life at one time. Find the words you want for guiding your every step and make it your mantra.

Bring out your wand. Let your inner fairy godmother create magic to sustain and define your journey of change. You have that power.

24

Guided Energy

With Guided Energy, you get to quiet your internal chatter, take a deep breath, and go on an inner world journey.

In this state of mind, you can release some of the anchors from your outer world to discover a new perspective.

You can gently visualize and empower the changes you want to make in your life.

You can also listen to this on YouTube.
Jeanne McElvaney Provoke Your Promising Potential

Or use your smart phone QR Reader

Provoke Your Promising Potential

Find a quiet moment when there will be no interruptions. Get comfortable. Take a deep breath and allow yourself to go to a place of no time.

Imagine a lovely, inviting door just beyond these words. The colors, shape, and texture invite you to turn the handle and walk through...

and you find a sunny meadow on the other side.

You step on a soft, grass path lined with colorful wildflowers. As you step forward, you realize this is the place you have been planting seeds for your garden of change.

Walk into your garden and see which dreams and new intentions have started growing. Take a moment in this place of no time to realize you are watering your growing blossoms of change by giving them your attention. You fertilize them when you use your imagination to envision more. Different. New.

As you move among the rich foliage of the changes you are creating in your life, you notice a large bag at the edge of your garden. It intrigues you... feeling both familiar and mysterious. Walk to the bag and open it.

It is filled with the energy of your potential.
Reach in and feel that energy. Let the sensation move into your hands and then soar through your body.
Smile.
Enjoy.   Allow, accept, embrace it.
This is the energy that is weaving into the changes you are making.

Open the bag wide and let the energy of your potential flow out. Witness its glory. Beauty. And power. Watch it flow outward into the energy field knowing it will move exactly where it needs to go to support you.

Bring your attention back to this page. Remember that creating changes using energy is a gentle journey of ease and joy.

25

Listen to Your Choir of Emotions

Every feeling is a valuable, essential voice as you sing your song of change.

In Old Thinking, our emotions are often seen as good or bad, positive or negative, even acceptable or unacceptable. Quantum Thinking recognizes their power to help us create the realities we desire.

Our feelings are messengers from our inner world. They are energy conversations between our awareness and the other 95% of feelings, beliefs, and thoughts beyond our awareness. When we pay attention to our emotions, they become guides from the place inside that is encouraging us to open our lives to wonder. While we might want to avoid a feeling like anger, it is there to help us recognize the need to adjust. Emotions are our truth-keepers. They point out imbalances.

Our state of mind is a powerful force of nature that moves energy. Dampening this force is like sitting in a car with the gearshift in neutral. All emotions shift us into change. Sadness can help us slow down. Guilt might encourage a new direction. Hope often takes us to new roads. When acknowledged, emotions are indispensable road signs as we journey with change.

Our feelings increase our self awareness. They tell us how we fit in any situation. They are the gauge we use for responding to people and give us invaluable information for making choices that honor us.

One of the deepest wounds of my childhood sexual abuse was suppressed feelings. I survived by ignoring any emotion outside being a *nice girl*. My healing journey showed me how my contained feelings kept my world small. Every time I identified, nurtured, and expressed a new emotion, my world grew; it expanded, delighted, challenged, and invited until I dared to sit down and write my first book.

When you are ready to put your change into high gear, go to the Internet and find a long list of different kinds of emotions. Read them and notice which feelings are uncomfortable for you to acknowledge and express. Recognize they are clues to what blocks the shift you want in your life. Start nurturing a new relationship with them.

*Go to your emotions. They hold answers beyond your awareness. They are your allie*s.

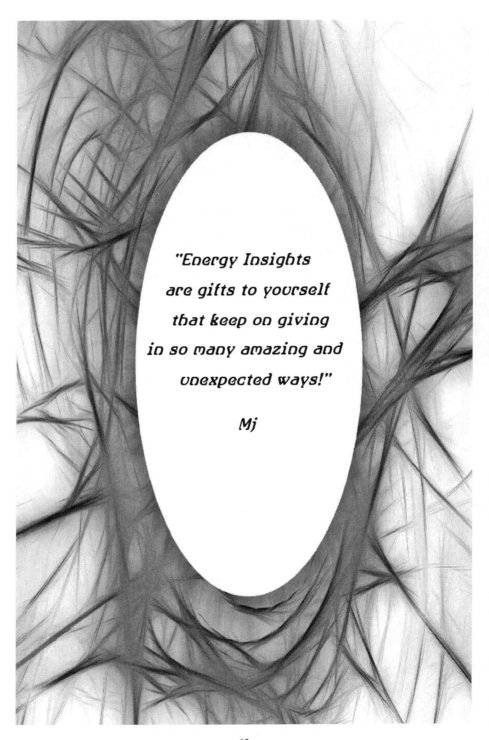

"Energy Insights are gifts to yourself that keep on giving in so many amazing and unexpected ways!"

Mj

26

Childhood Abuse and Energy

1. We have an energy link to everything we've experienced.
2. To change how we feel about ourselves and the way we fit in the world, we have to release emotional energy rooted in our past.
3. Thinking about past trauma or subconscious triggers create the same energy pattern we experienced in that moment, causing the same biochemical response.
4. We can't recognize new possibilities when we're energetically connected to thoughts, feelings, and beliefs of our past abuse.
5. Healing happens when we find words to process our abuse and recognize how we felt disempowered in that moment... from the perspective of the child who experienced the abuse.
6. Suppressed, dissociated, and unexpressed emotions are stored in every cell of our body.
7. Unhealed abuse keeps us in a constant state of stress energy.
8. Trauma is stored in the primitive part of our brain and can be accessed with energy.
9. Leaving logic and reason behind and stepping into the landscape reflecting our inner world uses the boundless connection to the unlimited knowledge held in the energy field.
10. Personal truth has the power to heal.
11. We can trust the child within us; he or she is the truth-keeper waiting for us to listen.

27

Adore Your Truth

Truth is a fluid energy. It takes shape under the influences of experience, perspective, and emotions. In any circumstance, there's his truth, her truth, their truth, and your truth.

We empower change when we find the color of our truth. Consistently responding with what resonates for us creates a strong network of unconscious responses that support shifts.

The energy of our truth is tangled with what's true for others. It's the nature of energy. Truths connected to our inner circle are wrapped around us like strong threads of a cocoon. Seeking change with energy allows us to respectfully untangle any threads that are limiting our personal growth. It's not about love, pointing fingers, or betrayal; it's about sorting through the different truths to see what serves us.

Honoring our truth inspires us to release feelings of selfishness. Taking care of our needs becomes an extension of living in a way that reflects our personal truth. As we express our authentic self, Quantum Thinking reminds us that each of us is creating our own reality. Our choices don't diminish others. When they come from our truth, they serve those around us as well.

Embracing our truth creates confidence to look closely at our lives. It's a guide for changes when we see things that no longer serve us. It also allows us to measure our experience against what we believe is important rather than matching our choices with what others think.

When my husband and I were moving, we consistently heard that we'd never find the house we envisioned in our summer-tourist home town. **As I heard these truths, I accepted the caring intentions and recognized I would not use them.** Instead I fully attached to my truth: I create my reality. In the middle of June, we found a house in town that had everything we wanted.

Your truth defines and celebrates you. It empowers change with its purity of intention. Encourage its place in your life. Throughout your day, start asking, "What is my truth?". Keep asking until you recognize how it feels. It's often a solid sensation like the trunk of the tree rather than the branches that move in the breeze of what others believe.

Our personal truth is the source of our authentic self. It's a guiding force that is always steering us toward our own cloud nine.

28

Guided Energy

With Guided Energy, you get to quiet your internal chatter, take a deep breath, and go on an inner world journey.

In this state of mind, you can release some of the anchors from your outer world to discover a new perspective.

You can gently visualize and empower the changes you want to make in your life.

You can also listen to this on YouTube.
Jeanne McElvaney Vanquish Stale Self Perceptions

Or use your smart phone QR Reader

Vanquish Stale Self-Perceptions

Find a quiet moment when there will be no interruptions. Get comfortable. Take a deep breath and allow yourself to go to a place of no time.

Walk along a safe, inviting woodland path. Feel soft grass beneath bare feet.   Listen to the sounds.   Look to your left, noticing the details.   Let the lovely air wrap around you as you revel in the fragrance and let the colors entrance you.
Be fully in the moment. This is your retreat. Your place of no time.

As you continue along the serene path, you find a deep, clear, still pond. Walk to the edge, lean over, and look into it. You'll see yourself reflected in the quiet water.
  Notice that what you usually see in the mirror's reflection becomes even more beautiful. You glow as your inner world is reflected back to you. You're aware of seeing what is magical, mystical, and wonderful about you.
      This is who you are when released from your usual thoughts, beliefs, and feelings.

Look deeper, past the image that is reflected and into your pure energy.
  Enjoy your reflection transformed into vibrating energy of color, light, sparkles, and shimmers. Notice how your energy appears in this moment... then watch it expand into the entire pond until there is no sense of water. Just vibrating energy.

Step into the pond, knowing you are leaving any energy behind that no longer serves you. It simply collapses on the shore as you gently step forward and wade into the energy that celebrates you.

Notice any messages that come from the pond as you wade, feeling safe and comfortable. Trust whatever comes to you. It's your energy sharing something insightful. It's something that will gently nudge you forward.

Bring your attention back to this page. Remember that creating changes using energy is a gentle journey of ease and joy.

29

Feel It. Be It.

It's who we are "being", not what we're "wanting" that creates reality shifts.

Quantum energy is both waves of possibilities and particles of matter. The waves flow with unlimited potential until our thoughts, beliefs, and feelings form a clear energy pattern of connection. In that moment, the wave collapses into our reality.

Moving our focus to possibilities can overcome our resistance to change. Doors open when we recognize that our current reality doesn't reflect how it is. It's just what we've come to expect. *Never* and *Can't* are mere illusions while we wait until we are ready. Feeling it and being it encourages us to wade into the deep pond of change while feeling safe near the familiar shoreline of what we know.

Acting as if we're already experiencing our desire supports change. Our new reality can feel as if it is happening right now if we stay enthusiastic, let inner joy guide us, and expect manifestation. We can wear new clothes, talk about ourselves in fresh ways, and use time differently. In these ways, we reinforce the change we're seeking.

Change is empowered by new actions. We can do something every day to stimulate the shift we're seeking. When we find ways to practice *being* what we want to experience, we encourage old feelings to fade and a new sense of ourself to grow. Like Cinderella dressing for the ball, we allow optimism to shape the future.

The quantum field responds to body language and facial expressions. I consciously use the power of this energy. When I want to be it, I might watch my posture or walk with confidence. When I want to feel it, I'm likely to smile often or look for something to happen that will translate into joyful surprise.

Tweaking your focus can help you *feel* and *be* the change you want to experience. Connecting to things at the edge of what you want will fine tune your new energy pattern. If you want a vacation, focus on seeing new sights, meeting people along the way, identifying what needs to be done before you go, tasting new food, or feeling excited.

When we change our experience, we transform our inner world where our feelings, thoughts, and beliefs create new energy patterns that will become our reality.

30

CHANGE YOUR STORY

THE FEELINGS, THOUGHTS, AND BELIEFS WE SHARE WITH FRIENDS AND NEW ACQUAINTANCES ARE POWERFUL ENERGY FORCES THAT DIRECT OUR FUTURE.

We're all story-tellers. It comes naturally as we talk to others about our life. Quantum Thinking helps us understand that our stories aren't simply reflections about what has happened or is happening. They are a compelling source for change.

Our stories are potent because we are so emotionally attached to them. We feel like they define us. Even if the chapters are filled with complaints, worries, doubts, and fears, we don't rip out the pages; they feel essential because they explain how we got to this current moment.

Altering what we share about ourselves may feel like we're being less than truthful, but doing this is a magic potion when it comes to change. In quantum living, nothing is absolute. We're constantly moving through shifting possibilities that are interconnected. When we change our story, we change the pattern of energy that is creating our experience and shaping our future. We initiate a life shift.

The reality we're now living is serving us in some way. It's important to honor what we've created. At the same time, we get to choose which stories we want to weave into our future. Whether that story is for ourselves, family, friends, or acquaintances, it is forecasting what will happen. If we recognize there is something that no longer feels like a good fit, we get to drop it. If we want to have more of the same, we can continue repeating that story.

When I dropped my laptop and lost the first seven chapters of a recent manuscript, my husband listened to my lament. I felt comforted as I talked about my daunting challenge to move forward. That's when he had the courage to ask me if this was the story I wanted to feed into the future. **I treasured his reminder of my power to create my reality.** His hugs were lovely, but his question helped me change my story as I began rewriting an even better manuscript.

Each moment gives you an opportunity to recognize what you are willing and ready to have. Watch what you say. Be aware of what you are repeating and emphasizing. Keep editing your story so that it outlines the future you want to create.

You are the author of what is to come. That's the challenge. That's the fun.

31

An Energy Dialogue for you ~

I created Energy Dialogues because they invite active conversations with energy.
They provide new perspectives.

These dialogues never insist you take action. No guilt or 'shoulds' come with them. They come as encouraging allies to expand your possibilities.

These simple interactions with energy help you tap into the 95% of your feelings, thoughts, and beliefs that are beyond your awareness but continue to drive your choices. They are playful, making change an adventure with a new guiding voice.

Talk Forward

Determination is often the first ally we call on when we want to change. Like Watty Piper's *Little Engine That Could*, we step forward with, "I think I can. I think I can. I think I can. I know I can."

This Energy Dialogue will connect you to a more powerful force of change: success-energies from past experiences.

Stand on one side of a room, clear your inner chatter, and fully focus on the shift you want to make in your life. Maybe you want more free time. Perhaps you dream of making money with your creativity. You might want to go back to school. Feel your personal desire in your body, thoughts, and feelings until everything else fades away.

*Notice that when you think of taking steps toward your desire you immediately connect to reasons it can't work. They invade your thoughts like ants at a picnic. Your dialogue challenge is to ignore them and connect to all the reasons you **can** succeed.*

Recall one other moment in your life that you dared to try something new and made it happen. Learning to ride a bike? Getting a job? When this memory comes, let the empowered energy of that moment flow through you. Revel in the sensation. Then take a step forward.

Do this again. Find another time you succeeded when challenged. When you remember, feel the energy and take another step forward.

Imagine the change you want is waiting for you on the other side of the room. Keep remembering other times you've experienced your personal power to make things happen. Let the feelings, thoughts, and beliefs of that moment wash over you, and then take another step until you've traveled across the room to your change.

32

Seek Energy Messages

Energy is constantly "texting" us. We can call on its wisdom at any time by opening up to the stream of communication from the quantum field.

We're empowered when we notice unusual happenings. Those quirky moments we often shrug away are energy shifts supporting our change.

An energy message feels like unexpectedly catching sight of a best friend though a window of a passing train while traveling far from home. It's a distinctive, resonating interruption that penetrates an ordinary moment. Our inner chatter pauses. Our focus shifts. Our gut responds. The out-of-context message may not be clear, but you know something just happened that changes your perspective.

Our quantum "text" can come in many forms. You'll recognize that it's a message because it nudges you in a new direction that serves you. You might be watching a movie and, out of the entire dialogue, one statement stands out. Vacuuming, you get a flash of a rug you've never seen but feels like yours. Perhaps, at your favorite coffee cafe, a woman wearing purple tennis shoes makes you feel inexplicably sad.

Strangers, family, and friends can also be messengers. Soon after my beloved dog passed, I took my first trip to do errands without her. It was a challenging, emotional time for me. As I stood in line at the local fruit stand, I felt numb. When I stepped up to the counter, the air around me thinned. I knew from experience this meant a message was coming. The cashier looked into my eyes and said, "It's time to play."

Enable your journey of change and read oracle cards. These purchased decks come in many themes. Their purpose is to give you positive, metaphysical insights, and they are a fun way to get messages from the energy field. You can draw one each day to read empowering and encouraging passages. Or you can draw a card when you have a question.

Energy messages remind us we're using Quantum Thinking to make changes. They connect us to an invisible web of far-reaching information. By letting go of Old Thinking that gives us 7 bits of information, we tap into the 40 billions bits of insights available in the energy field.

Like Easter Eggs, messages are tucked into every corner of our lives. If we seek them by paying attention, we shift change into high gear.

33

Talk to Energy

All of us have a best friend who is aware of our every thought, feeling, belief; she is energy. Wise and responsive to our needs, she knows our life purpose and is an empowering muse walking beside us.

In the clamor of our emotions, the chatter of our thoughts, and parade of our beliefs, the whispers of energy insights can get easily lost. Talking to energy helps us connect to the generous information in the energy field.

The language of energy doesn't ask you to learn any new skills. The first step is to quiet the clamor, the chatter, and the parade in your mind to the best of your ability. Then silently ask a question or focus on something you want to know more about. The energy field will respond with images, metaphors, colors, emotions, or physical symptoms. Like any new language, it takes practice.

Your greatest challenge will be to trust what comes to you. When you talk to energy, you are tapping into information from the 95% of your thoughts, feelings, and beliefs that are usually beyond your awareness. Be prepared for answers you don't expect and remember they will always be FOR you.

As you talk to energy, you are empowering the changes you want to make. Quantum Thinking will no longer sit with the dust bunnies on the top shelf of your maybe-someday closet. You are creating an interactive relationship that is playful and spirited. You are being reminded that you are working together to create your reality.

I talk to energy about everything, but especially when my days are taking me toward a new reality I'm envisioning. When I started writing this book, I focused on the manuscript, letting my usual inner chatter fade away. My body felt like it was being compressed, and I recognized I was feeling pressure. In that same quiet moment, I silently asked, "What is the pressure?" I kept repeating the question until I saw a clock with jumbled numbers, the minute hand spinning around. Talking to energy showed me that I believed I had to add this book to what I was already doing. I trusted this energy insight, and it helped me release that belief. It guided me to rearrange my days to honor my writing journey.

Energy is a chatty friend with information that physicists now know travels faster than light. With practice, we can have conversations with this gentle ally who offers unexpected revelations.

34

An Energy Dialogue for you ~

I created Energy Dialogues because they invite active conversations with energy.
They provide new perspectives.

These dialogues never insist you take action. No guilt or 'shoulds' come with them. They come as encouraging allies to expand your possibilities.

These simple interactions with energy help you tap into the 95% of your feelings, thoughts, and beliefs that are beyond your awareness but continue to drive your choices. They are playful, making change an adventure with a new guiding voice.

This, or That, or That?

We're constantly faced with practical, empowering choices we may not consider because we tend to react in ways that are familiar. It feels more reasonable and safe to use the beliefs, feelings, and thoughts that are part of the 5% floating in our awareness. This Energy Dialogue connects you to the unlimited field of information for answers that are connected to your deepest needs and desires.

Start with little choices. Work with decisions that aren't emotionally charged until you feel confident.

Imagine you are going out to dinner but don't know whether you want Italian, Mexican, or something you haven't thought of yet. Rather than letting a carousel of feelings and thoughts fill your mind, create three scraps of paper that are the same or use post-its. Write each choice on a separate piece of paper. Fold them. Mix them up and leave them spread out on a table while you go about your day.

Come back to them when you feel at ease. Quiet your inner chatter and focus on 'whatever serves me'.

Hold your hand above one of the pieces of paper. Notice how your hand feels. The energy from that eating experience will interact with your hand; you will be having an energy conversation. Energy will talk to you with a feeling of warmth, or tingling, or a sensation of your hand being pulled toward or pushed away. It may speak to you by giving you no sensation; that's also a message.

When you have observed the energy interaction, step back. Shake your hand or rub away the sensation. Then check the second and third choice in the same way.

Notice which choice gave you the strongest reaction. That is your energy insight about which eating experience to choose.

Making choices this way creates delightful clarity. Over time, you start seeing that you truly do feel served by the gentle nudge in ways you never imagined.

35

Pull Intuition Out of the Mystical, Magical Realm.

We tend to connect Santa Claus, Easter rabbits, tooth fairies, and intuition together. All of them a bit amazing, mysterious, and delightful as they share unexpected gifts.

Intuition is not a magical moment from another realm. It's an insight coming from the constant communication that is natural in the energy field.

I'm often asked how you can be sure you're having an intuitive hit. Practice will help you recognize the difference between your thoughts and energy communication. Listen for the whisper. Watch for sudden clarity and certain knowing. Trust what you know. You'll find intuitive hits are unique and consistent for each of us whether it's a physical sensation, vivid emotion, or flashing image.

Intuition is a constant energy ally when we turn down the volume of our thoughts, feelings, and beliefs. For this book, I'm inviting the uncommon insights of my intuition: I want it walking beside me. Knowing it's an energy that most often whispers, I'm consciously inviting its wisdom by creating quiet moments in my days. Driving, sitting on my front porch, taking a shower, I see my thoughts, feelings, and beliefs as channels on a television, and I turn the volume down so I can hear what might come.

Intuitive hits come more often when we trust what we hear.
My intuition feels like a best friend, and I know it will confide in me more often if I respond to its messages. It's easy to shrug away insights that so often seem disconnected to what is happening in the moment, but if something in my days stands out for any reason, I pay attention to the information. I know it's there to guide me to the best outcome.

Intuition is a tool that can be used any time we choose.
When I first recognized intuitive information was available in every moment, I began making it part of my life using little, unimportant choices and questions. That made me feel safe as my confidence grew. Now, it's a trusted, lovely ally in all I do. When I started writing this book and got a Facebook message from a stranger who celebrated my writing, I recognized the energy field was encouraging me. When I'm faced with choices, I like to write each one on a piece of paper. I wad them up and mix them around. Then, one at a time, I hold each one in my hand. I know one of them will feel like it's being held in a bubble of light air because my intuitive hits always come with that feeling. The way you get your hits will be different than mine, but they will feel the same each time they arrive.

Shifts we want to make are empowered by our intuition. The information is protective, empowering, and encouraging. Learning to hear the wisdom is the challenge and the fun.

36

Explore Why You Created Your Current Reality

At any time, our life is the culmination of a series of changes. Each of them took root with an insight that was followed by action.

We create our experience as our thoughts, beliefs, and feelings meld into a cohesive force that feels more real than any input from our five senses. The reality we manifest makes us feel safe, empowered, and loved.

We are in continuous energy shifts guided by the 95% of thoughts, feelings, and beliefs that are beyond our awareness. This is where our emotions are strong and clear, the very thing needed to create changes. To interpret why we travel paths we don't like / understand / want to discard, we can look for answers within our emotional inner world.

Old beliefs hold a wealth of information about our current reality. Family stories, subtly and persistently woven into our perspective, are a rich source of influence. Past social groups, communities, religious connections, and schools created impressions that are foundations of our current experience. There's evidence that beliefs can be rooted in our genes from past generations. All old beliefs can serve us or get in our way. Sorting through them can give us life-changing insights.

Childhood emotional wounds are the drumbeat of our reality. Our cells carry these energy scars that continue to direct our choices when we are adults. Until we heal by seeking our personal truth and using our voice to acknowledge our experience, our wounds are in charge. We can change the rhythm of our reality by exploring what has been buried then energetically releasing the child still caught in the web.

Being aware of Old Thinking helps me understand why I created my current reality. I grew up thinking determination, hard work, will-power, and a good plan were the elements that would shape my life. I continue finding these gremlins hiding in the corners of my endeavors as I turn to Quantum Thinking to bring about a reality shift.

You are experiencing what you believe is possible. Your current reality is a reflection of what you created using your truth. With energy insights and action, you get to change. You get to add more dimensions, more bangles and bells, and more color, joy, and inspiration to the reality you're creating.

Being aware of our reality encourages energy shifts. Questioning our reality sets change in motion.

#37

An Energy Dialogue for you ~

I created Energy Dialogues because they invite active conversations with energy.
They provide new perspectives.

These dialogues never insist you take action. No guilt or 'shoulds' come with them. They come as encouraging allies to expand your possibilities.

These simple interactions with energy help you tap into the 95% of your feelings, thoughts, and beliefs that are beyond your awareness but continue to drive your choices. They are playful, making change an adventure with a new guiding voice.

Pass Unwanted Energy Back

Our life journey includes experiences that stick like jam on our fingers long after we've eaten toast. Our thoughts keep circling back, revisiting past events. Tangled energy from a time of high emotion hijacks our attention.

If your experience was uncomfortable, upsetting, or unpleasant, this Energy Dialogue lets you consciously release the tangled energy. If your experience was traumatic, this Energy Dialogue can soothe, giving you a new perspective that will encourage healing.

Stand in a quiet space that ensures no interruptions. Hold your hands out in front of you, palms up, as though someone were giving you a bowl. Let yourself recall the moment that keeps recycling and 'see' it as energy; it might be a dark ball, dense fog, red lightning, wilted flowers, or a yellow tornado. Trust what comes to you.

When you 'see' the energy, imagine it filling the bowl in your hands. No matter how big the energy is, it fits, and you can feel the weight of this burden pushing down on your hands.

With the energy from that moment now gathered, turn around. Imagine you are now facing the source of your tangled energy ready to send it back to the experience where it belongs. Silently talk to yourself: "This energy no longer serves me, and I release it."

'See' the energy flowing out of the bowl and moving into quantum space until it disappears. Feel the bowl get lighter until there is no weight and the bowl is gone.

Turn back around.
Take a moment to connect to the present, your feet firmly planted on the ground.
Notice how you now stand taller and feel stronger.
Let the freedom of release fill your body. Smile.

38

Follow your personal spirit

We have an energy that is intimate with our feelings, thoughts, and beliefs. It carries the blueprint of our life purpose. It communicates with the energy field. I call it personal spirit.

Quantum Thinking encourages us to celebrate and honor 'who we are' and 'can be' rather than who we think we 'should be'.

Our personal spirit gathers information and pollinates what celebrates the core of our being. It's always seeking to align our inner and outer worlds. Feeling like the love of puppies, the loyalty of dogs, and the resiliency of wolves, it allows us to give up struggles and lean into soul-filled insights.

When we're in a stormy sea of challenging choices, our spirit is our lighthouse, guiding us to our personal truth. Using the blueprint of our life purpose, our spirit encourages us to see what serves us and weaves it into the changes we seek.

Constantly communicating with the energy field, our spirit thrives on energy shifts. When we find ourselves following one path while another intrigues us, we can be sure our spirit is guiding us. While we are focused only on what we can see, it knows the span of our journey. It gives us freedom to express our authentic self.

When I met my husband, I told him I "had no spirit." He didn't challenge me, believing my journey would reveal what he perceived. It did. My spirit, a creative, supportive, powerful ally emerged as I healed from my childhood sexual abuse. Though I felt myself turned inside-out, soft, sure confidence spread into every area of my life. My passion was born; I had to help others connect to their own beacon.

Invite your spirit to be part of your days. Picture this omniscient, calm, caring force as an orb of energy in your body. Visualize it connected to your inner wisdom and the quantum field. See it as an information operator plugged into unlimited resources and ready to link you to them. Listen to the gentle whispers that ring true. Let them guide your choices.

Our personal spirit is a swirling core of energy that holds all knowledge and connections that make us beautifully unique. It's there to help us shine.

39

Expect Serendipity

The joy of unexpected happenstance.
The delightful surprise.
These are also tools
in creating change in the energy field.

Old Thinking tells us serendipity is about luck, a fluke, a rare coming together. It's people and circumstances randomly connecting, leaving us feeling touched by the mystery of life. When you are using energy to create change, you recognize serendipity is part of the journey.

Quantum Thinking reminds us that we move toward experiences we have launched with intention. The moment our anticipated outcome becomes a focus of our thoughts, feelings, and beliefs, the energy field begins responding. It lines up circumstances and people who can empower our intention. As matching energies start streaming toward us, we experience serendipity.

The shift we've set in motion responds, and we are more open. Like putting our car lights on high beam, we notice more in the periphery of our days. Connections that would have gone unnoticed or seemed insignificant now catch our attention. Possibilities that can become part of our change arrive, and we have a joyful jolt of serendipity.

When I had completed my first novel, getting published felt a bit like taking myself to Mars. I was completely out of my element but determined and open. That was when my husband and I were asked if we would fix a shower door for a friend's mother. I hadn't seen Marcelle for years and was delighted when our catch-up conversation brought me serendipity. In talking about her writer's club, she mentioned the name of a local publisher who was open to first time authors. That led to the publication of my first book.

Serendipity confirms that the energy field is responding to your intention. Notice how often this kind of energy weaves through your days. Let it encourage you. When it arrives, enjoy the sensation and then take action. It's bringing you opportunities to support the energy shift you intend by showing you new energy patterns in your current reality.

You empower your intention when you <u>expect</u> pleasant surprises. Change can be fun when serendipity is opening doors for you.

40

Uncover Clues in Conversations

Notice which discussions engage you. Listen to what you are saying. When you are aware of what you're saying and encouraging by agreement, you are connecting to a powerful tool of change.

Because we instinctively crave the comfort of having our world view confirmed, we seek conversations that agree with our beliefs, thoughts, and feelings. These conversations aren't passive; they are creating our reality.

Our conversations show us where we're taking our life. If we stay aware of what's being said, we can use it as a guide. When we want more of the same, we let the discussion flow. If we don't want something following us into the days ahead, we deflect it.

Even casual conversations can be the start of change by pointing out our view of the world. Are we commiserating about the trials of life… and feeding that forward? Are dreams, desires, and intentions on the table… celebrating the unlimited possibilities in the energy field? When we note the mood of a discussion, it can tell us what we are encouraging in our life. It can be a road sign guiding us in a new direction.

Conversations reveal what we believe is possible and expect to happen. They are incredibly insightful opportunities that can make us aware of how our inner world is guiding us. It's a chance to learn about ourselves, so we can change.

I'm often shocked by what I hear myself saying… or *almost* saying. **In these moments, I know that what I consciously believe, feel, or think is colliding with what I hold at a deeper level.** I see this as a huge opportunity to recognize something that is affecting my reality. Then I get to work with this phantom power until my conscious and subconscious world reach agreement. This makes it possible to create change without the block of this internal conflict.

The next time you have a conversation, recognize that there is an invisible ally present; energy, constantly communicating beyond time and distance and with all other energies, is listening. Its natural inclination is to respond to all you are sharing. You could say it's taking notes so it can know what to bring to you.

Our conversations are the crayons we use to color future days. Choose colors that celebrate the life you want.

41

An Energy Dialogue for you ~

*I created Energy Dialogues because they invite active conversations with energy.
They provide new perspectives.*

These dialogues never insist you take action. No guilt or 'shoulds' come with them. They come as encouraging allies to expand your possibilities.

These simple interactions with energy help you tap into the 95% of your feelings, thoughts, and beliefs that are beyond your awareness but continue to drive your choices. They are playful, making change an adventure with a new guiding voice.

Tuning into Your Chatter

All of us have about 40 thoughts each minute! Most of it's gossip about ourselves. As we make changes in our lives, inner opinions very often rain on our parade.

Most of the chatter goes unnoticed, but it's still a strong force in guiding our choices. In this Energy Dialogue, you become an active participant in this usually one-sided conversation.

To become aware of what you are saying to yourself, create pauses during your day and then listen to your last thought. You might do this whenever your phone rings, when you see the color green, or when you walk into your kitchen. Choose a pause that is connected to something you do often during the day.

When this moment comes, consciously recall what you were just thinking. Don't emotionally attach to it. Just take note of it. Ask yourself if the thought is supporting your change and taking you into the future you want.

If the answer is yes, stretch the thought into a paragraph of feelings and beliefs that reinforce it.

If the answer is no, take 15 seconds to tap your upper chest and say, "I'm releasing thoughts that no longer serve me."

42

Repair Your Reactions

Our state of mind sends constant emails to the energy field, and that field replies with positive support to every message.

Reactions are spontaneous reflections of our inner world. Based on established beliefs, thoughts, and feelings, they are energetic connections that will bring more of the same unless we change.

How good can it get! When we're facing a challenge and another thing doesn't go as we imagined, we are inclined to shake our head and wonder *'how bad can it get'*. Asking *'how good can it get'* switches our thinking to new possibilities. It creates a different energy outcome.

Yes. Yes! Yes. How often have you experienced something wonderfully unexpected and uttered, "I don't believe it." In that moment you are declaring your limitations. You will transcend old expectations if you immediately stop that response and say, *"Yes. Yes! Yes."*

"Thank you. Thank you, thank you, thank you." I'm often muttering this to myself. It's a way to be aware of the many positive, little things that happen during changes. Non-responses and being on automatic pilot is another way we communicate with the energy field; it gives us more of the same. *Thank yous* can make us more proactive.

"What do I need to know?" Quantum Thinking has taught me physical symptoms are messages from my inner world. I no longer associate them with illness. Instead, I respond by asking, "W*hat do I need to know*?" When I experienced a retinal tear, I immediately started asking this question. My inner wisdom whispered, then made it clear: it was time to *be*. All my *doing* was making it harder to listen to my personal spirit. My eye challenge didn't change my sight; it changed my life path. Listening to my body is one way I have changed my reactions to empower shifts.

"More please." This response sends a powerful message into the energy field. Like your wish-list for Santa Claus, it encourages you to imagine more and think about what you want. It celebrates **you** thinking about **you**! It urges you to make your needs important. It helps you put yourself first.

Positive reactions are magnetic, joyful ways to empower new realities. They help us be aware that we are shopping in the store of life and can make affirming choices.

43

Identify Your Tribes

Energy patterns respond to feelings, thoughts, and beliefs. They are the Pied Piper's flute bringing people together.

Our tribes are many. Like overlapping circles, some people may share several tribes with us, but no two people have exactly the same combination. We're much too marvelously unique for that to happen.

Within every social group, energy always mingles. At school or work, we're responding to purposeful energy. Circles of friends react to our inner world or common interests. All our tribes have their unique value. We empower our ability to create new realities when we realize these bonds fluctuate. That means, as we change, our tribes will strengthen, modify, or fade in a way that feels very natural.

When we feel free to share our most authentic self in a tribe, our connection to contentment, love, and happiness increases. The support we experience is energetically linked to the 95% of our feelings, thoughts, and beliefs beyond our awareness. It goes beyond shared interests and similar lives. This is the tribe that helps us thrive and the one we want to seek when we're changing.

New friendships give us a unique energy group. Friends from the past are like photo albums holding energy patterns that reflect our journey. Recent friends see us from a fresh perspective. As energies merge into a new tribe, we often open up to emerging desires.

Like trampolines, social groups feel most balanced when everyone stays steady. Yet personal changes will shake things up. We are empowered when we focus on the new possibilities we're bringing to our tribes. When I remarried two weeks after meeting my husband, I brought new thoughts to old conversations. They had the chance to meet a new friend. As my world expanded, so did theirs.

Your tribes are a reflection of how you see yourself. They provide safe reinforcement for the beliefs, thoughts, and feelings of your current reality. When you use other people's responses to guide your choices, you're using Old Thinking, and everything will stay the same. Change is empowered when you identify your tribes and check to see if you feel free to explore possibilities outside the circle.

Tribes are a constant source of feedback. Like Goldilocks, we serve ourselves when we check to see if our social groups are 'too big', 'too small' or 'just right' for the changes we desire.

44

Transcend Blocks

Change is often the child of buoyant revelations; it feels inspired. Yet many changes come from the frustration of personal blocks.

Blocks are infused with protests: I've done everything I can think of ~ I'm doing my best ~ I'm doing all I can ~ You don't get it / see me / understand. In this murky energy, it's hard to remember we can choose to create new energy patterns that will bring change.

Old beliefs become blocks when they start making us feel trapped. Change seems like unraveling the very stitches holding the fabric of our life together. Yet this kind of block *can* make us start moving toward the glow we sense at the edge of our days. Inertia pushes us to set our own goals, and we gain optimism as the energy field responds to our new desires.

Feelings are often the blocks in our lives. They can pull us into familiar, upsetting patterns even though we want to soar. They can make us feel disempowered. When we're stuck in emotional cycles, we can connect to change with symbolism. We might carry a significant stone, light candles, or feel release through breathing exercises.

Sometimes, our blocks are giving us a safe place to hide. My personal path has been strewn with such havens. They are always backed up with solid reasons and excellent excuses, but change doesn't happen here. Quantum Thinking has helped me see blocks as indicators of my commitment. Does it make me feel like, "Whatever it takes!" If so, I step into my reality shift with heart and soul, and the block melts.

You wouldn't be alone if your block is about getting lost in another person's energy. It's the surest way to put your dream in a holding pattern. You react and respond to *their stuff* rather than daring to reveal the tender shoot of your own desire. This block is an energy you created in the past to keep you safe. Challenge it with updated information. Transform it with insights. Try focusing on yourself.

When our potential is buried deep inside, we feel blocked. We can release the fluid and flexible energy of potential by tapping into our needs. When we *want* something, it feels optional. *Needing* something feels essential, and this creates a pure, strong pattern of energy that ignites change.

When considering your dreams, don't feed the troll under the bridge. Let Quantum Thinking be your shield and sword as you move past.

"Listen to the mustn'ts. Listen to the don'ts.
Listen to the shouldn'ts, the impossibles, the won'ts.
Listen to the never haves, then listen close to me...
Anything can happen, child. Anything can be."

"Listen to The Mustn'ts"

by Shel Silverstein

45

Slip into a Place of No Time

In the quantum field, time doesn't tick to a constant beat. It's an energy that curves inside-out, backward, and forward. It blends the past, present, and future to shape our current experience.

Ticking clocks and passing time are a convenience we've created to manage our lives. They are a fantastic tool in our daily lives but can become a weed in our garden of change.

In the energy field, information is constantly being passed among our future, past, and present. Our future communicates with us. We can step off the train-of-time that makes our destination feel like it's off in the distance. Doing this opens us up to the insights and resources from everything that was and will be. Quantum Thinking allows us to slip out of time.

We can't leave our past behind. We *can* change it. Every time we change our emotion, we affect what has happened. Quantum Thinking gives us opportunities to transform experiences that continue to make us feel diminished, disempowered, scared, and ashamed. We can untangle previous energy connections by using our thoughts, feelings, and beliefs to align ourselves with the energy shifts we desire.

We set the time frame for how long it will take to make changes in our lives. Energy exists outside the dimension of time. Quantum shifts can happen in a single moment, a week, or a month. Releasing our concept of time allows us to recognize we are choosing how our energy shift will unfold.

Quantum time affects our energy shifts. I try to catch myself when I initiate change and believe it will take time. I also honor my need to let shifts unfold slowly, recognizing it gives me an opportunity to adjust. When something happens 'out of the blue', I try to remember my previous thoughts, feelings, and emotions set it in motion. I know that five minutes can feel like an hour and that's **real**... it's quantum time.

Every time you change, you are reshaping both your past and future. Grab that opportunity. Let your awareness feed this glorious, magical, marvelous facet of the energy field. Take off your watch, turn your clock to face the wall, and actively release your old connection to time. Don't let time be the conductor of your choices; allow your personal rhythm to write music that will soothe and inspire.

Slip into a place of no time often because this is where your personal spirit dances beneath rainbows.

46

Look into Love's Kaleidoscope

Love is more than an emotion; it's an energy. Initiating change encourages us to look at love from a new perspective.

We unconsciously seek experiences to support our beliefs because they create a surge of feel-good energy. All emotions are biochemical memories of experiences, and our sense of love was embedded long before we could examine the shapes and colors of this feeling.

Redefine love. We tend to believe love is expressed by giving away pieces of ourselves. Saying 'yes' to every request and taking care of unspoken needs can feel like the beam of this energy. As we look through the lens of Quantum Thinking, we might decide this emotion is the nectar we share when we're growing our potential. It could be the abundance flowing to others as we tap into our personal power.

Love might be expressed in choosing to be an honorable witness. Though worry is often considered an offshoot of caring, it's an energy that feeds doubt. Quantum Thinking reminds us that empowering thoughts can be an expression of love. In this way, we celebrate each person's unique journey. We recognize and honor their challenges as part of creating, refining, and exploring their own reality.

Love of personal growth is an animated ally for change. It's the kind of energy that followed Dorothy and her friends down the yellow-brick road. Though it challenges our desire to turn back to comforting, old beliefs, it's balanced by our brain's passion for learning. With this kind of love, we get to look through our kaleidoscope and see endless, changing colors of new possibilities.

As we take a look at love, we may realize it's not a deep, still pond. This energy flows like a river, rushing around opposing life values, settling into like-minded coves, forging promising tributaries, and mostly flowing steadily. Every change we embrace, affects this force. If we move to a new community, love that was previously a strong thread may give way to a blossoming love for the new view out our window or the fantastic cafe just down the street. Love changes, grows, and explores just like we do. Recognizing this and making choices with this in mind, can ease resistance when we initiate energy shifts.

Love is like weather, a force both beautiful and complex.

47

Be in Balance

Making the impossible possible is as normal as a leaf floating on a gentle river. Energy flows toward least resistance.

Our body is the perfect tool for inviting balance into any area of our life. With energy, knowing what we want doesn't mean we have to <u>make</u> it happen. More often it's about finding easy ways to experience <u>the feeling</u> we're seeking.

Use your body to speak the language of equilibrium. Stand on one foot and focus on a spot in front of you, using the wall for support if that helps you feel steady. You're creating a physical sensation of balance that is being translated into the energy field. You're practicing being in the shift of balance you desire and opening that flow into all areas of your life.

Focus on new emotions. Put your arms over your head and reach as high as you can. Consciously send energy up and out of your body. Imagine the following words flowing into the energy field through your finger tips: Love. Inspiration. Passion. Optimism. Openness. Change. Release. Allowing. Trusting. These are emotions that feed quantum change.

Connect to your inner world. Reach your hand over your head and lean to the right. Be aware of balancing yourself. Know that changes in your body affect your beliefs just as your beliefs alter your body. Change position; reach your other hand over your head and lean to the left. Remind yourself that quantum change takes root in your inner world.

I like the unique balance I experience doing the yoga Warrior pose. I say, "*I am a warrior woman*" and see myself passing through a portal where all aspects of my life are in beautiful harmony.

Maybe you've already created a nest of time that feels balanced and reflects your deepest needs. Although your days may not look like those of people around you, the pace, commitments, and activities feel right for you. On the other hand, if some aspect has started feeling too big and heavy or too scattered and scarce, use your body to connect to balanced energy; invite equilibrium to spread into all areas of your life.

Our mind loves associations. Balance your body, and your thoughts will very naturally join the energy field in creating harmony in all areas of your life.

48

Fortify Changes with Creativity

Creativity is all those things we do in our own special way. It's abundantly woven into our days. Consciously using this natural inclination reinforces change.

Creativity breaks old ties to what we believe is reasonable and practical. It's attached to feelings of happiness and exploration... and these are energies that invite change.

Quantum Thinking reminds us our outer world is a reflection of our inner world. Like the clothes we wear, creativity is an expression of our lovely, lively individual energy. When we pay attention to our unique take on things, we can get insights that will show us how to adapt changes in ways that feel fulfilling.

Our creativity gives us opportunities to face our doubts, own them, and let them be part of our shift. Original endeavors are littered with the unexpected. What we thought would work doesn't. Initial goals are reconsidered. These are the moments we let go of plans and move in another direction. We can bring this gift of flexibility to the changes we are making.

In the energy field, the strongest energy connection is emotion. Doing anything that makes us smile ignites the change we desire, and creativity is driven by what feels good. Our originality delights, empowers, and celebrates us. These feelings convert energy waves of potential into new realities.

For me, playing with words is a powerful force of change. I love how each word stands alone creating a response. And then! I get to play with single words, stringing them into sentences, rearranging them, rhyming them, or finding active, adaptive, artful alliterations. This creativity reminds me that shifts don't follow a path. They are often about rearranging my life.

Seek your own creativity. Recognize how many ways you express your unique view of things. Be open to the possibilities it encourages. Notice how warm and fuzzy and empowering your creativity feels. Feel its flow. Hold on to these feelings and let them be a guide for the changes you're making.

Creativity expresses what we are exploring in the 95% of feelings, thoughts, and beliefs beyond our awareness. It's an inner world experience that builds a bridge between what makes us unique and what we have in common with others.

"Inside all of us is a wild thing."

"Where the Wild Things Are"

by Maurice Sendak

49

Acknowledge Energy Bubbles

We have an energy bubble around us that both connects to and limits interactions with other people. With our feelings as sentinels, our bubble establishes the space we need to feel comfortable as we explore and experience changes. Though unspoken, it lets others know how we want to interact.

Changing our feelings automatically alters our choices and that transforms what happens between ourselves and others.

Happiness expands our energy bubble. This momentary feeling has the power to help us identify experiences that celebrate our personal spirit. It confirms we're on our authentic journey. Remembering this energy is not a state of being, that it pops up between challenges, we can stop feeling bad when it's not present. We can embrace both the expansive times of happiness and the more contained, personal moments.

Anger makes a sharp-edged bubble. It creates detachment that can help us see circumstances more clearly and have new insights. While it pushes people away, this change in our energy creates emotional safety when needed. It can connect us to our intuition and empower shifts in our life.

Excitement electrifies our bubble. Feeling exhilarated opens us up to unrestrained connections that encourage change. The responsive, communicating nature of energy zeros in, and we sense a oneness that is shared with those around us. We're aware that anything we can imagine is held as an energy wave of possibility.

Fear is a reflective bubble. Quantum Thinking confirms that our experiences are an extension of our mind. This bubble mirrors our inner world even while it's an ally pointing to potential external dangers. Fear allows us to guide our people choices, knowing we can disconnect energetically as well as physically.

Inspiration will make your bubble magnetic. It makes you feel connected to a future that celebrates you and invites like-minded people into your days. To bring more inspiration into your life, notice quirky moments in conversations and experiences. When that almond flour catches your attention while shopping, let it lead you on a merry chase that appears to have no purpose, and you will be experiencing inspired living.

Like the Cheshire cat, our energy bubbles appear and disappear, leaving us with a smile as they encourage us to embrace the space we need to grow.

50

Adjust to Others

Like Jack and the Beanstalk's single bean, the influence of others is something much bigger than we imagine.

In the invisible, intelligent, always communicating quantum world, we are not separate from others. Unconsciously, we are being affected by each other, and this thread weaves its way into our changes.

We are empowered when we recognize others affect our shifts. Who activates our energy? Drains it? Neutralizes it? Discerning this isn't about how much we care. It's about taking note of which energy connection will help our newly budding change.

We seek relationships that share similar realities. This can inadvertently disempower change. Sympathy validates our experience and maintains old energy patterns. Others can love, care, and wish the best for us, but their comforting, familiar energy can make the search for the best of ourselves more daunting.

Comparing ourselves to others makes no sense in quantum change. Each of us is creating our own reality to feel safe, empowered, and loved. What others are experiencing can point out a shift we want to instigate, but no one has something we can't have; we just haven't imagined it, or it hasn't yet matched the energy patterns of our inner world.

I see others' experiences as a potential menu for my own possibilities. If they have something that appeals to me, I let it guide me into a new reality. When styles changed to oh-so-comfortable leggings, seeing others wear them helped me change. I chose to buy them in spite of how I thought I'd look. I let the realities of others help me challenge old beliefs.

The moment you believe your experience is *caused* by other people, you are giving them your power. It's hard to remember *you* create your reality. To remind yourself, do something out of the ordinary: wear mismatched socks, paint your nails blue, hang a picture upside down, eat with your fingers. Remember, you get to be your own fairy godmother of change. That's the challenge. That's the fun.

We are part of an ocean of energy with others. They affect us. We affect them. Shifts happen as we respond to them. Their shifts are connected to ours. Adjusting to the interactive flow is part of our journey into change.

51
POKE AND PROD LABELS

WE AUTOMATICALLY LABEL EVERYTHING BECAUSE OUR MIND THRIVES ON ASSOCIATIONS. IT SORTS AND CATEGORIZES EVERY PERSON, EXPERIENCE, AND SENSATION THAT TOUCHES OUR LIFE.

Waves of possibilities are at the core of quantum living. That's exciting. It can also be overwhelming, so, to soothe ourselves, we instinctively label the information we process. Those labels can limit us.

Changing the label of a feeling can change our reality. We tend to believe emotions are turned on like a faucet; when something or someone interacts with us, it gets turned on, and our feelings flow out like water. That's Old Thinking. Quantum Thinking reminds us our feelings are generated in our inner world, named by our mind, and used to respond. If a friend misses a lunch date, an old emotion-label might be, 'She's mad', but we can choose to relabel what we're feeling with something that serves the reality we want to be experiencing: 'I'm glad she knows I'll understand.'

Labeling comes as easily as breathing. We stereotype others by outward appearances, behavior, even energy connections. It's a response that can feed our changes or starve them. Are the labels part of our current beliefs? Will they fit in our new reality? Do we want to avoid or explore what the label tells us? Is it time to erase the label or add an exclamation point? Becoming aware of labels and sorting through them empowers us.

I am still poking and prodding the labels around my potential. I'm leaving a trail of discarded judgments as I move forward. I often imagine standing next to a stream with old labels falling on me like rain. When one sticks, I look at it to see if it honors my journey and intentions. If it does, I put it in my pocket. If not, I rip it into pieces and toss it into the stream where it becomes fish food.

The labels you give yourself become post-its you wear to get confirmation from the outer world. Have fun using a pad of post-its to redefine yourself. Write one word *you'd like to be* in your new reality then recall a moment when you experienced being what you desire. It's there. Let it bubble up. Use your inner world to confirm this new label and then stick it onto your clothes. Do this until you're wearing a new identity. *Who you think you are* is creating an energy pattern that is shaping your future.

Being conscious of the labels we're using lets us be our own Mary Poppins of change.

52

Practice Placebo Healing

Our body is energy: pure, vibrating, communicating molecules. Its natural inclination is physical well-being.

Shifts are affected by our physical comfort and welfare, and we have infinite effect on how good we feel.

The placebo effect is extremely powerful. In a test at a Texas VA hospital, a simple incision created the same results as actual surgery for patients who believed they were having their knees treated. Even more intriguing, researchers who are weaving Quantum Thinking with medicine have found placebos work even when we know they are being used. We can consciously use harmless choices for healing.

Our health can improve when we associate specific behaviors and thoughts with our well-being. We can take vitamins because they are recommended, but we increase their potency by focusing on how they support our body. Rather than swallowing a Vitamin C while thinking about our day's schedule, we can rev up the effectiveness by thinking about what it is doing for us.

Because of Old Thinking, most of us need action and something visual to believe we are healing. For that reason, we get better results with placebos that make us do something. Any choice will work as long as it feels real and requires effort; our sore wrist will heal more easily if we wrap it than if we just send it positive, healing thoughts.

Symptoms are messages from our subconscious. When my knee became stiff, I knew it was trying to tell me something. I asked what I needed to know, and, clearing Old Thinking, I listened to the energy message. *Walk into my writing* came to me. When I responded by committing to a new writing project, that effort became my placebo, and my knee settled back into its usual, flexible comfort.

If you are experiencing symptoms you don't want, Quantum Thinking encourages you to look at old beliefs you have about your health. Past experiences, what you've been told, and family truths have a powerful effect on your well-being. Held in all 60-80 trillion cells of your body, old beliefs drive your responses for taking care of yourself. Sorting through them to see which ones serve you will put you in the driver's seat.

Our thoughts are not observations; they are architects of our future experiences. Placebos can be the structure for changing our health.

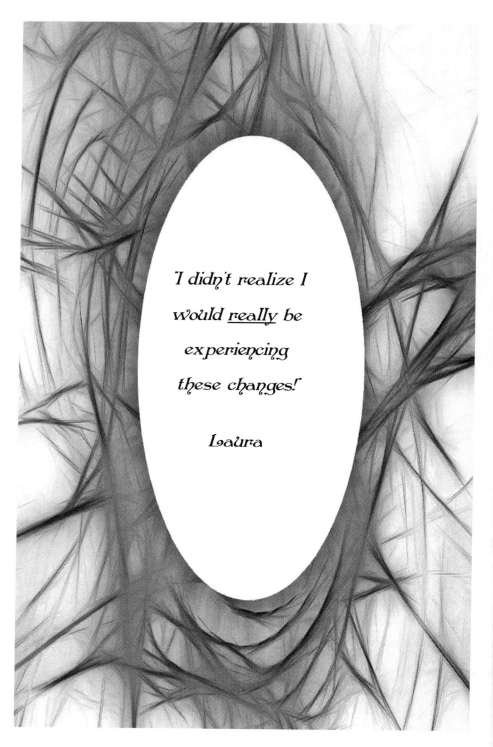

"I didn't realize I would <u>really</u> be experiencing these changes!"

Laura

53

How Energy Is Connected to Healing

1. When we hurt ourselves, we can direct our thoughts to positive, empowering beliefs and feelings that change the outcome.
2. Memories of similar moments will tend to reproduce similar experiences, and we can change that by focusing on quantum beliefs around healing.
3. Our body stays the same if we feel the same.
4. Quantum thinking encourages us to sift through the information we accept and believe. Being told side effects, listening to television ads, even signing releases before surgery, have the potential to change the reality we create around healing.
5. Thoughts and emotions create body responses and symptoms.
6. Society's messages affect our relationship with health and well-being.
7. Most of us believe healing is a gradual experience, but in the energy field it doesn't have to be.
8. Our bodies and emotions are always energetically connected.
9. Quantum Thinking reminds us that old beliefs can link family health cycles, but our genes are changeable. They are influenced by our experiences, stress, emotions, and learning.
10. Energy insights and experiences can be a powerful ally as we work with medical care-providers.
11. All living matter is in continual change.
12. Spontaneous healing is normal in the quantum field. We can tap into it by: balancing the energy in our lives > remembering we are part of the energy field and connected to energy waves of possibilities > recognizing the emotion that is at the root of what we're experiencing > finding ways to feel bathed by healing energy > giving ourselves permission to heal > remembering that healing is our body's natural response > creating behavior we believe will heal us > changing our belief about what we expect to happen.

54

Guided Energy

With Guided Energy, you get to quiet your internal chatter, take a deep breath, and go on an inner world journey.

In this state of mind, you can release some of the anchors from your outer world to discover a new perspective.

You can gently visualize and empower the changes you want to make in your life.

You can also listen to this on YouTube.
Jeanne McElvaney Bathe in Well Being

Or use your smart phone QR Reader

Bathe in Well Being

Find a quiet moment when there will be no interruptions. Get comfortable. Take a deep breath and allow yourself to go to a place of no time.

Stare into these words and then beyond... focusing on the lights around this page. Feel both connected to what your are reading and distracted by the lighting around you. Relax. Release. Let go of any thoughts chattering at you right now.

In your mind's eye, look beyond the lights and out into the Universe. Imagine looking deeper and deeper, moving past sparkling stars until you notice a vibrant white ball of energy in the far corner.

Focus on the ball. Feel its gentle power. This is an orb that is holding your unlimited potential for healing. Take a deep breath and feel it respond to you. As you continue breathing deeply, the energy ball moves toward you. It moves through the Universe and into the space around you. It feels friendly. Lively. And as you nod, it moves to the top of your head.

Feel its warm tingle and notice it transforming, moving into your head like nurturing spring rain. Let this warm, massaging energy flow through your head, down your neck, and into your shoulders. Follow the white, sparkles of energy as they continue a massaging flow into your chest, moving downward and filling your body with healing, white light. Feel it move through your pelvis. Down your legs. And into your feet where it pools and tingles... bringing a deep sigh.

Now see the healing energy moving back up through your body, knowing it carries healing energy for you. Let it bathe your body with well-being. Feel its warm power reaching every part of your body.

When it reaches the top of your head, invite this energy to stay with you... flowing through your body with its very natural healing.

Bring your attention back to this page. Remember that creating change using energy is a gentle journey of ease and joy.

55

Recruit Energy Buddies

In the fluid energy field, change comes with sunny giggles and surprises. A circle of insightful, inspiring pals gives us an umbrella in case it rains.

Energy buddies can point out, nudge, and redirect us during our journey of change. They help us keep track of the joyful feelings that come with energy shifts.

Knowing someone who is interested in personal growth using Quantum Thinking is a bonus. During change, both our old and new realities exist. Our challenge is focusing on what we want while the old energy pattern fades away because we aren't giving it our attention. Our energy buddies can help us stay focused and excited during conversations. They can alert us to Old Thinking.

Affirmations are energy buddies that keep us from getting lost in busy days. Like a lighthouse, they can be a guiding beacon to help us navigate old responses that would take us off course. If an affirmation is, "I release all worries and embrace my potential", it can't overcome our subconscious beliefs and feelings. It won't create a reality shift, but it can help us remember our intention to make changes that grow our life.

Choices are energy buddies that help us remember we are in charge of our change. Each choice has a particular energy pattern that will either resonate with our inner world or not. They give us options that we can try on. If they are a perfect fit for what we need and hold dear, we'll feel like Winnie the Pooh finding honey.

My body is one of my most appreciated energy buddies because it's in constant communication with my inner world. If I'm over-scheduling, my body will accept the flu bug that is going around, strongly suggesting I take a break. When I'm making a decision, I consciously use body language to empower myself. Instead of sitting when I'm considering my options, I stand tall with my hands reaching for the sky. That creates different thoughts.

Every change begins with your imagination. Feed it. Hug it. Poke it. Snuggle and dance with the mental images that tickle, and they will open doors to what you want. Make your imagination one of your very own seven dwarfs to mine your possibilities.

About 90% of our thoughts are recycled every day. They dominate in creating our realities. Energy buddies can help us overcome this army of influence.

56

Work With Words

Words have an almost magical ability to reach the very core of each person. Whether heard or spoken, they are the stuff of superpower.

Like call-numbers on library books, our mind organizes information using associations. Any word, like 'mom', 'mud', 'maybe', will connect us to a group of thoughts that create a personal energy pattern. That pattern goes into the quantum field to create our realities.

Power is a stormy word. Emotions of every variety pour through us when we connect this word to change. We feel its weight, want its transforming capacity, and can be scared of using it. This internal tug-of-war can hinder shifts unless we find a very personal definition that makes *power* a friend and comfortable ally. For me, *power* is pushing past limitations I've created and daring to share what is best in me.

'My' can deceive us. When it comes to change, this word can declare something belongs to us that may not be a good fit for our intention. We might say, "*My block* is lack of time." This isn't something we want, but, by owning it, we become unconsciously and energetically attached to keeping it. We would flourish more easily if we used "*this block*".

Mystery is a magnetic word that can attract or repel us. Though many of us love the intrigue of the unknown from a distance, we tend to avoid subjecting our own lives to enigmas. Change thrives when we snuggle into the inevitable moments of mystery that come with it. Wearing the optimism of *rose colored glasses*, we can let curiosity take us to previously unknown places and embrace the mystery.

Food is a word I have worked with in my journey of change. With Old Thinking, I saw it as a source of gratification. Quantum Thinking showed me it was more; food became my body energy buddy. Now I don't shame it, make it the enemy, or abuse it. We work together finding choices that celebrate what serves my physical well-being and still satisfies my chocolate cravings and burger-with-fries desires.

Make songs a change companion. Music can forcefully mobilize your inner yearnings. Notice lyrics of old favorites that encourage growth. Open up to meaningful words and phrases that soar through you, encouraging you to believe there is more. Consciously use music that touches you. Let it be your personal anthem.

Finding words that describe the change we want will bring that desire out of our inner world. It will activate our intention.

"Life is like riding a bicycle.
To keep your balance you must keep moving."

Albert Einstein

"Reality is merely an illusion, albeit a very persistent one." Einstein

"If at first, the idea is not absurd, then there is no hope for it." Einstein

"Imagination is more important than knowledge. For knowledge is limited to all we now know and understand, while imagination embraces the entire world, and all there ever will be to know and understand." Einstein

"Play is the highest form of research." Einstein

"It is an optical illusion that we are separate." Einstein

"Everything is energy and that's all there is to it. Match the frequency of the reality you want and you cannot help but get that reality. It can be no other way. This is not philosophy. This is physics." Einstein

"Space and time expand, contract, and warp in 4-dimensional curves, looping back on itself." Einstein

"The intellect has little to do on the road to discovery. There comes a leap in consciousness, call it intuition or what you will, and the solution comes to you and you know how or why." Einstein

"If you want your children to be intelligent, read them fairy tales." Einstein.

"The woman who follows the crowd will usually go no further than the crowd. The woman who walks alone is likely to find herself in places no one has ever seen before." Einstein

"The most beautiful experience we can have is the mysterious." Einstein

"Don't wait for miracles, your whole life is a miracle." Einstein

57

Take Charge of Tangled Energy

All energy is connected to and affected by other energy. This brings bright opportunities. It also presents challenges.

Encourage expansive, lucid contemplation, so you can see everything as part of an interacting life flow. When we are making changes, remembering this can empower us.

Everything is energy, and all energy is *tangled* in a vibrating, communicating, interwoven oneness. Quantum research has confirmed we aren't physical beings separate from the energy field. Consciously connecting to this all-knowing, nurturing intelligence, we can use it as a counterbalance to the uncertainties of change.

Our feelings are energy, and so they get entangled too. When we are sharing our emotions, we are sharing energy. In initiating shifts, it serves us to consider which energies will help us. An optimistic friend can tip the scales toward change. A friend filled with loving worries and concerns will weigh down new intentions. When we're creating a new reality, Quantum Thinking reminds us that everyone's emotions are getting tangled in our effort.

We experience an energy exchange with everything and every person that has our attention. If we're seeking a new job, our strongest focus will create the most powerful connection. We can use that knowledge to create the outcome we want. Thinking about our old job will energetically bond us to it. Fixating on a new job can drive our friends crazy, but it will enmesh our energy with what we want.

When I wanted to trade-in our gas-guzzling, older truck at a financially challenging time, common wisdom said we wouldn't qualify. **I chose to tangle my energy** with a small, gas-efficient sedan. I completely dropped all thoughts about our truck and had long, on-going chats with myself about the car I wanted and the monthly payment that suited me. Much to my husband's surprise, trust in quantum changes brought us the car three weeks later with the payment I had been imagining.

You can stimulate shifts by releasing outdated, tangled energy. If you concentrate on what you desire, you'll find past entanglements will wither. This focus will you bring you firmly into the present moment and this is where new possibilities bubble.

In the same way Cinderella's glass slipper brought her together with the prince, entangled energy is a force of connection.

58

Smile

Smiles warm our hearts, acknowledge a shared moment, and invite connections and intimacy. They can also activate change.

When we feel good, the energy message races to our facial muscles, and we smile. It's also true that, when we smile, we energetically communicate with our body and make ourselves feel good. This is the place to be when you want to create an energy shift that warms your heart.

Smile energy has a unique pattern that will connect you to different possibilities. If you dress yourself in a smile and go to the library, you will pick different books than if you walked in unaware of the energy you were wearing. The librarian will treat you differently. And don't be surprised if you get back in your car and find that thing you lost earlier in the day. That's the kind of experiences you invite when you choose smile energy.

Although my morning began with a computer challenge, I chose to smile as I opened my manuscript and started writing. It's the kind of energy I want to share in this chapter. I also know the energy I hold as I write this book is shaping my experience as an author. I don't want that experience wrapped in challenge. I want it bubbling with smiles.

Many people feel that choosing to smile is not sincere. That's Old Thinking from a cause-and-effect view of the world. We now know a smile can be a tool in creating changes. You get to smile and be reminded of what feels good to you. Then let that emotion weave into your thoughts and bathe your beliefs with warm, fuzzy feelings from your soul. As you shape your future with change, you get to create a feel-good foundation.

Smile right now! Just smile for no good reason at all. Smile and look up from your reading and notice how different your surroundings feel. Be aware of what catches your attention. If there are other people in your space, observe how they respond. You are witnessing an energy interaction that goes beyond body language.

Your smile has power. It may be bubbly, warm, calm, delicious, open, friendly, loving, even optimistic. Whatever feelings your smile elicits, you can be sure they are positive energy for the change you want. Use your smile as your North Star.

59

Observe Your Change

Quantum changes may arrive with fanfare and a parade. More likely, they will slip seamlessly into our lives and be subtly satisfying.

By paying close attention to what is happening when we are manifesting, we add fuel to the fire of change. Conscious awareness of the process is a way of saying, "Yes!" to the energy field.

Our friends often notice nuances we would miss. In the middle of figuring out how to use a new computer program, one friend might be impressed that we're attempting such a thing. Another friend might point out that we're smiling more. I notice a glow around friends who are in a shift. These reflections can help us recognize our progress.

A sense of well-being is part of the journey. Being open to change and taking steps to make it happen create feelings of success even before we experience our new reality. The courage to show up, seek help, allow new possibilities, express hidden talents, and share our inner world unleashes a sense of well-being.

Anticipate the inevitable surprises. If we don't experience the unexpected, we are using old paradigms to create our reality. In every moment, all possibilities exist. Unforeseen events confirm we have imagined our way to something new. They are the delightful spices in our soup of change.

What's <u>not</u> happening is part of our energy shift. When I started doing energy work, I imagined both classes and personal sessions. My logic declared this a great idea. As my personal sessions blossomed and my classes withered, I saw that my inner wisdom was guiding the change. With no classes, I have honored my need to write this book.

You'll have moments when you feel your change isn't happening. Don't feel discouraged. Your energy shift won't unfold in the way you imagined; it won't seem logical or respond directly to your expectations. Determination won't be in charge. Quantum change uses connections that feel more like a bit of magic and fairy dust; you won't arrive at the exact destination you expected, but ***it will feel*** like what you originally intended.

If we carefully tend the seeds we plant in our garden of change, they will thrive.

"And all the colors I am inside

have not been invented yet."

"Where the Sidewalk Ends"

by Shel Silverstein

60

Nurture Your Dreams

Our dreams are dark chocolate, delicious energy. They feel a little bit unacceptable and, thank goodness, they keep enticing us. In spite of what we might have been told, they nourish us.

Long before we decide to change, our desires set shifts in motion. They keep breaking through "the practical", "the reasonable", "the too busy", asking us to imagine. Our task is to foster the kinds of changes that will make our dreams possible.

Commitments are a safety net we establish in our life. They create structure, strengthen bonds, define us, build our future, and empower us. Like a vine, they are an energy that spreads. We rarely question them unless they begin to overrun our garden of life or start strangling budding possibilities. Our dreams are encouraged when we make sure old commitments are still a good fit.

Change is often about releasing, as much as it's about creating something new. Like our homes, our lives can sometimes use a *spring cleaning*. Remember, everything is energy. We can look into our days and see what is gathering dust: a routine, a habit, a responsibility, even knickknacks, pictures on the wall, or holiday decorations. Anything we can leave behind, opens up energy space for something new. It massages our dreams.

Gratitude can be a way to lift our dreams out of someday. When we identify what feels good in our life, we're also connecting to energies we want to feed into the future. We're making a mental list of realities that are a perfect fit for our dreams and are connected to happiness. To set a dream in motion, expand your statements of gratitude. Instead of, "I appreciate my children," say, "I appreciate my children and the way they support my dreams."

We've learned to navigate the river of our life, but our dreams are invigorated when we toss the oars and follow the currents. Dreams ask us to go beyond our expectations. Going with the flow of life requires the same thing. Give your dreams a chance to grow by embracing what comes your way rather than pushing it away because it's not what you had in mind. If you're given a Lavender Peppercorn ice cream cone rather than your usual cinnamon coffee, accept it. Taste it. See if you've been given an opportunity to change. You can decide it's not for you, but, meanwhile, you have just nurtured your dreams.

Be your own Christopher Columbus. Challenge common knowledge and dare to explore the unfamiliar landscapes... of your dreams.

61

Guided Energy

With Guided Energy, you get to quiet your internal chatter, take a deep breath, and go on an inner world journey.

In this state of mind, you can release some of the anchors from your outer world to discover a new perspective.

You can gently visualize and empower the changes you want to make in your life.

You can also listen to this on YouTube.
Jeanne McElvaney Summon Your Haunting Dreams

Or use your smart phone QR Reader

Summon Your Haunting Dreams

Find a quiet moment when there will be no interruptions. Get comfortable. Take a deep breath and allow yourself to go to a place of no time.

Step onto a warm, white-sand beach. Wiggle your bare feet. Feel the massage of the fine sand as it moves around your feet. This is your beach, your time. In your mind's eye, stretch. Feel the serenity.
  Feel pleased. *Safe.* *Embraced.*

Feel the sun gently kiss your face as you look out into the timeless, blue ocean. Notice a glass ball bobbing up and down close to the shoreline.

It calls to you. *Intrigues.* *Pulls on your heart.*
  Wade into the gentle, warm water and pick it up.
    Notice how it feels oddly soft with layers and layers of transparency.

Your spirit soars as you realize you can look into it, like a crystal ball.
  You look closer and find a deeply held dream of yours clearly reflected. It may be a new dream. Or an old one that has been set aside. It may surprise you.
  Trust what you see.
  It's a dream that is ready to create a change in your life.
  The time is perfect for you.

As you hold the orb in your hands, it begins to feel warm. Let that warmth flow into your hands and through your body. This is your dream energy. Smooth... tingling... and inviting, it's a perfect fit. Be with it until you are ready to come back into the present moment. See if it brings you an insight or message.

Bring your attention back to this page. Remember that creating changes using energy is a gentle journey of ease and joy.

"**If you keep on believing, the dreams that you wish will come true.**"

"Cinderella"

by Charles Perrault

62

Keep Going

Change can catch us sitting on the fence. "Do it" and "go for it" hum within, and we <u>Know</u> we'd be happier if we jumped. But Old Thinking keeps nagging us about the challenges – unaware of the almost magical way Quantum Thinking makes change unfold.

When we create change using energy, the perfect experiences and people find us. Synchronicity and unanticipated support naturally feed our intention. We can depend on that if we keep taking steps into change until our 'old normal' no longer feels 'normal'.

With quantum change, there is no predetermined destination. The journey feels more like traveling in a glowing sensation, and we get to be a "Curious George". We get to ask the energy field to confirm our progress. This empowers our intention by keeping us connected to the change we seek. Looking for proof helps us recognize *coincidences* that are feeding what we want.

Creating quantum change is so much about awareness. Old thoughts give us more of the same. So does distracting ourselves. To keep going, we're served by creating or looking for ways to remind ourselves of our intention. We can rearrange an item we use daily, like our toothbrush. We can tune into ways a movie, book, or song feeds our awareness and let these be joyful ways to remind us of our journey of change.

Changing our mind moves us forward. It lets us use what we learn along the way and respond to our unfolding shift. With quantum change, staying steady with our original intention doesn't serve us; it only keeps the energy circling around current progress. Honoring our new needs and desires, as they reveal themselves, empowers us.

People who encourage change keep us moving forward. When I moved my focus from being a grandmother to writing, I felt I left my grandson behind. Then he sent me a school paper he'd written about the people he most admired. I was there, for daring to try something I'd never done before. He changed my perspective and inspired me to continue honoring my reality shift.

When you're changing, the seedling of your new reality is going to be surrounded by weeds of Old Thinking. You'll pull a dozen weeds for each seed you plant. Every time non-productive thinking pops up, replace it with blissful, optimistic thinking about your shift. Remove the weeds with imaginings and possibilities.

Keep going. Like Cinderella's mice transformed her with a gown, the energy field responds when we keep our dream alive.

63

Make Your Life Purpose Important

Each of us arrives in this life with a treasure to share. It's an energy that seeks expression and is connected to our joy and contentment.

There's an ache, an itch, a puzzling restlessness that keeps urging us to share our unique gift. It doesn't rest until we swim in the energy of our purpose. Then we're inspired, deeply connected, and expressing the best of ourself.

Like an itch in the middle of our back, our purpose can feel hard to reach even though it's persistently on our mind. Deep down, we *know* we have a talent, an idea, or a way of expressing ourselves that has the power to make a difference in the lives of others. Even deeper, we know it's important to find our way out of what keeps us contained. A first step is giving ourselves permission to be *more*. That opens the door for movement through the energies of self-consciousness, shame, fear, and embarrassment.

Our passion was ignited by life experience. We're driven by our need to share our experience and bring change to others, rather than a desire to be a hero. Believing in our purpose erases conflict between our inner wisdom and Old Thinking. It increases our sense of happiness and makes our challenges feel like growth toward our best self. Whether it's planting a garden or rescuing a child, we do it effortlessly, expecting nothing. It feels timeless. It makes us smile when no one else is looking.

Restlessness swirls inside us when we can't define our purpose. We know something essential to our thriving is missing and feel limited by seeing our possibilities through usual thoughts and conversations. Using our relaxed state as we fall sleep or first wake up, we can let our mind wander and ask, "What would be wonderful for me?" Though it can feel unrealistic, letting 'wonderful' be our guide will give us insight. Trusting what comes to us will bring an answer.

Your purpose is too unique, too personal, to be found on a well-trodden path. You can embrace it more easily by nurturing a craving for the unknown and remembering the energy field holds unlimited possibilities. Start small on this journey and look for ways to see usual choices through new eyes: you might wake up early to discover what dawn offers, you could buy a book about an unusual but intriguing topic, or you can do *that one thing* you've always imagined doing.

Emerge from your cocoon and be your own butterfly.

64

Guided Energy

With Guided Energy, you get to quiet your internal chatter, take a deep breath, and go on an inner world journey.

In this state of mind, you can release some of the anchors from your outer world to discover a new perspective.

You can gently visualize and empower the changes you want to make in your life.

You can also listen to this on YouTube.
Jeanne McElvaney Gossip With Your Future Self

Or use your smart phone QR Reader

Gossip With Your Future Self

Find a quiet moment when there will be no interruptions. Get comfortable. Take a deep breath and allow yourself to go to a place of no time.

Imagine making plans to meet a long-time friend you've lost track of. Think about a lovely, perfect place to have a conversation. Feel the anticipation of what is familiar and deeply connected. Let the excitement of your always-insightful exchange bubble up.

Setting aside all the things on your mind, go to the place you've chosen, knowing your friend is already there.

That friend is your Future Self. It's you in the joy and completion of the solid change you've created. It's you feeling empowered. It's you feeling a genuine connection to the gifts of your new reality.

As you greet your Future Self, notice her vibrant well-being... how she now dresses... her confidence... her energy. Greet her with a hug and smile. She knows you well. She knows your challenges. Today, you get to ask her any questions about the changes you are creating.

Without trying to figure it out, being totally open to any response, ask her what advice she would give you. Listen to the answer, knowing it's not a call to action. There's nothing you have to do with the information. It's just an energy insight.

Ask her what surprised her as she manifested your desire.

Ask her what she had to release to create an energy shift.

Sit with your Future Self and share your thoughts and challenges in the moment. Listen to what you are saying for more insights. Then thank her for coming to you today with wisdom of passing time.

Bring your attention back to this page. Remember that creating changes using energy is a gentle journey of ease and joy.

With energy, you can see past the surface into the root of what is holding you back... Challenges can be seen from a new perspective. New realities can be created. Practical, life-changing tools are available.

Do you wonder if Quantum Thinking can work for you? This is what the following people experienced as they explored changes using energy in personal sessions or group sessions. ~ Jeanne

Duchess's Energy Experience with Her Health and Well-Being

When you're with Duchess, you're in the presence of an abiding force with charming, ready giggles. She has overcome every obstacle spina bifida has thrown her way. Along the way, she's been a wheelchair tennis champion and surfer, the most athletic woman I know. But she was scared to death of her dental appointments; her health history had created medical PTSD.

After a life-time of relying on what she called, "her Big Brain", Duchess didn't dive into energy work. First, she needed information about Quantum Thinking. We let her empowering curiosity guide us in our sessions.

When Duchess recognized her deep dental fears were rooted in past, dissociated medical experiences, her perspective changed. Knowing that her emotions were being driven by old feelings of being at risk and disempowered gave her a basis for working with the challenge of getting her teeth cleaned.

To help her feel empowered, Duchess began by interviewing the dental team. We had identified three things she needed: to use her voice, to explain her medical PTSD, and to 'feel their energy'. When that went well, she made an appointment knowing she could stop the procedure at any time. This made her feel less at risk.

Duchess worked with the energy field as she waited for her dental appointment. Each time fear began to invade, she worked to break her Quantum Loop with active, persistent new thoughts. She created a powerful, beautiful image that she called 'the vortex', a place where she connected to the energy field's unlimited possibilities. Knowing her expectations were creating her future experience, she mentally rehearsed an appointment that made her spirit soar.

When she called me after she'd had her appointment, Duchess was all giggles and joy. She had an experience that changed her relationship with her dental health and well-being. For her, the challenge and success were as big as landing on the moon. It gave her "energy tools" to use when other medical situations followed.

Chevy's Energy Experience with Healing Childhood Sexual Abuse

When I heard Chevy describe herself as a "crone", I thought, a crone must be a timeless woman showing up in the world with her personal spirit fully expressed'. I *knew* it had to define a courageous soul because, for 25 years, Chevy had persistently followed a path of personal growth.

She came to me for a personal session because one of her childhood sexual abuse memories continued to haunt her. Even though, over the years, she had processed her teenage abortion performed by her abuser to fill in details and give her insights, the wound remained open and raw.

This kind of wound can be healed when a survivor goes into the timeless, intelligent, communicating energy field and experiences the abuse from the child's perspective. In a very aware state of deep relaxation, Chevy re-experienced what kept nagging her and found out what made her, as a teenager, feel traumatized. She felt disempowered because she couldn't use her voice to help herself. She felt at risk because no one knew how bad it had been.

Because everything is energy and everything that was or will be is also in the present, Chevy was able to change that moment. Teen Chevy got to use her voice and tell the caring, adult Chevy how bad it was. While processing the memory, Chevy was able to recognize she was still carrying the belief that she had to keep track of 'how bad it was' to make herself feel safe.

Abuse memories haunt. Beyond what we experience, what we learn in moments of trauma is stored in every cell of our body and affects our view of the world until we release it. Empowerment came when Chevy chose to use energy insights to release this old wound. Living in peace and joy, she continues her journey of personal empowerment while being a healer for other survivors.

Linda's Energy Experience with Codependence

Linda came to the weekend Gathering desperate to change her overflowing calender of commitments. Her big heart, spot-on perceptions, and passion to empower others were tying her down when she was ready to explore. Though she declared she *"didn't get what working with energy was all about"*, Linda electrified the entire group of women with her infectious humor, enthusiasm, and can-do attitude.

Because codependence comes from the core of good intentions and old wounds, energy insights are a powerful resource. They give us a different perspective when we are driven by a feeling that we are essential for the happiness and well-being of others.

After learning how to communicate with the energy field, Linda got to explore. When she connected to the energy of a completely free calender, Linda felt panic. When she connected to the energy of a calender marked with personal-wish days, Linda felt challenged. When she connected to the energy of a calender heavily scheduled with commitments, Linda described feeling, "comfortable, sort of peaceful". She learned that the 95% of her feelings beyond her awareness weren't in sync with what she was wanting. It was an insight that set change in motion. While these Energy Dialogues were intriguing, the next set was even more powerful.

Linda experienced how her "helping hand" was energetically affecting those close to her. Rather than feeling empowered, one of her sons felt like 'he was going in circles'. When she felt the energy of that same son without her helping hand but believing in him, the energy felt 'like the sun was rising, warm and strong'. It was an 'aha' moment of how good intentions can be enabling.

Linda found these silent conversations with energy riveting and long lasting. The physical sensation of different energies stuck. Self-discovery eliminated resistance. Being able to explore her codependence through Quantum Thinking made it an adventure about opening doors and seeing her world with new awareness.

Jason's Energy Experience with the Power of Self Awareness

Jason carried a full backpack of Old Thinking and beliefs he was ready to challenge. Talented, creative, but feeling wounded, he wanted to live in all ways that honored his personal spirit.

Using energy insights, Jason recognized that how he saw himself was affecting the way he perceived and interacted with others. Daunted but determined, he dared to explore his self-perceptions rooted in the emotional and physical trauma of his childhood. He gave himself permission to dig beyond his inhibiting family dynamics and truths.

In Jason's journey of change, the connection between his physical symptoms and life choices was revealed. He learned to listen to his body. His chronic back pain was his only connection to his stoic dad. In placing himself in situations that called on extreme physical endurance, he was repeating overwhelming childhood experiences.

With energy insights, Jason began making new choices. He stopped drinking. Eliminated caffeine. Changed his diet. Became a dedicated yoga student. Jason changed his relationship with himself: mind, body, and spirit. He found his authentic self. He wrote children's books, built furniture, and offered drum lessons. Each of these celebrated his spirit and erased a long-held belief that he couldn't make money doing what brought him joy.

When Jason talks about making changes with energy, he is passionate that it's "not about information." He says, "being aware and connected to my feelings when I'm making choices has changed how I show up in the world."

Kathy's Energy Experience with Beauty

Kathy hesitated to bring up beauty in her personal sessions. It felt vain and maybe even selfish. I knew it was a perfect energy adventure connected to her spirit.

Knowing Kathy's relationship with her personal beauty was rooted in the past, I took her back to the moment the belief about her beauty was planted. She was six-years old and wearing an ill-fitting dress at an important church event; she decided she wasn't pretty.

Though Kathy remembered the event, she hadn't recognized the anxiety about her appearance had followed her forward. She didn't realize she had continued seeing her body through the eyes of that unhappy, little girl.

While in the energy field of that moment, this gentle, loving woman was able to reach out to the child. She saw what a sweet, cute little girl she had been. Kathy got to take her little girl out of the moment and let her have a dress that made her feel special.

Healing old wounds always connects us to current opportunities to cement what we've just learned. For Kathy, it was her son's upcoming wedding. Rather than her usual avoidance around dressing up, Kathy chose to dress herself in all ways that would delight her six-year-old. She made new and different choices. She spent time and money getting what made her feel her most beautiful self.

At the wedding, Kathy's energy healing enabled her to hear and accept compliments about how she looked. Even more importantly, she felt pretty for the first time in her life. When I asked if I could tell her story, she responded: *"tell them how it has deeply changed me and continues to guide me."*

JIM'S ENERGY EXPERIENCE WITH HIS CREATIVE PATH

When Jim talked to me about a repeating an unwanted work pattern, I took him to an Energy Dialogue called Talking Forward. This Dialogue resonated with the enthusiastic, optimistic inner-explorer that guides his choices.

He went back to the first time he experienced jumping full-spirit into a project that ended with the original intention betrayed. While he wanted to tell <u>that</u> story, the goal of Talking Forward is to tap into the empowering elements of the same story. This helped him identify what feelings he wanted to use to create his future.

Like everyone, Jim had to search for the elements of his work experiences that felt empowering, positive, and honored his personal spirit. He sometimes felt irritated when I redirected his need to lean into old beliefs so he could find nuggets of truth he hadn't connected to before. Humor and curiosity were his delightful allies as Jim focused on "the positive."

Going inward to find life-changing insights, Jim saw how his bone-deep honesty and passion for possibilities served him. He recognized the little boy inside him was finally being heard. He released a Quantum Loop set in motion in his childhood family: you don't get to succeed using your inventive ideas.

Jim's energy experience opened the door to a new path that connected to his childhood dream: to discover healing potions in the jungles of the Amazon. Though Jim isn't exploring the Amazon, his creativity is charting new frontiers of health and well-being.

Bee's Energy Experience with Love

As each person in the group described what they wanted to explore with energy, Bee was decisive and clear. Her emotional honesty was backed by a brave, shining spirit. For her, love felt elusive. Even when someone said they loved her, Bee "couldn't feel it."

In group energy sessions, I often hear how empowering and healing it feels to be in a safe place where all feelings and thoughts are embraced. Bee had brought a very tender part of her life to us. Each participant felt honored.

All Energy Dialogues are silent experiences. The participant feels and witnesses the energy held by the other group members without knowing what it is until the Dialogue is completed. Working together, we created some Dialogues for Bee.

In our first Energy Dialogue, Bee got to witness how love energy was interacting with her personal energy; it was a strong, hovering presence. In the second Dialogue, Bee got to experience the energy of possible blocks that were keeping her from connecting to love. When she felt the energy of 'not being worthy', tears came. In that moment, Bee didn't know what the block was, but she knew to the core of her being she was feeling the energy of her resistance to love. During the discussion after the dialogue, Bee felt empowered and relieved by experiencing her personal truth.

The third Dialogue brought a break-through insight for Bee. Not knowing what each member of the group held for her, she moved from one person to the next feeling the energy. Each time, it was a feel-good sensation. Bee was glowing when she asked us what she had just experienced. That's when she learned each of us was holding the love of someone significant in her life.

When Bee physically felt these different loves, she had a reality shift. Her old belief of being unworthy shattered. She realized unconditional love had always been present, and now she could feel it.

Five Women's Energy Experiences with Menopause

With menopause, women reach a place in their life-journey that offers a different focus. They feel more determined, more able, and more intrigued about creating lives that reflect their authentic selves. For many women, energy experiences make the menopausal journey a time of honoring "Self".

Caroline felt overwhelmed and unseen in her marriage. With energy insights, she realized her current feelings matched those she experienced with her emotionally-absent father. Processing her childhood energy connections made it possible for Caroline to see her marriage from a different perspective. Like dominoes, this changed her choices, then her relationship with her husband.

Charlotte wanted to finally face her fear that she might be "a little crazy". Using energy to uncover her dissociated memory of childhood sexual abuse, she confirmed she was only experiencing triggers and flashes of that trauma.

Beth wanted to get off antidepressants. Under her physicians care, she began decreasing her dosage as we worked with energy to reveal the root of her depression. She saw how the death of a friend had continued to affect her view of the world from that moment forward. Energy insights, rather than antidepressants, became her allies.

Theresa came to energy sessions because she was nearing retirement and wanted to chart a course doing the things she'd long imagined. Energy insights helped her identify the most exciting path. She learned how to use Quantum Thinking to ensure her journey honored her spirit while opening doors she hadn't imagined.

After of life-time of trying to live up to her family's expectations, Mary arrived at menopause angry and hopeless. With energy insights, she realized anger was a messenger to redirect her choices. Her hopelessness dissipated as she used those choices to change her reality.

With energy, menopause becomes a life-changing "pause" filled with promise. At this time, different parts of women's brain are activated, encouraging them to explore and express their inner world. With energy experiences they get to do just that.

"If things start happening, don't worry, don't stew,

just go right along and you'll start happening too."

"Oh, The Places You'll Go"

by Dr. Seuss

If you liked this book!

1. Share your enthusiasm with a friend.

2. Gift the book to others so they can ignite their own changes:
   Order through Spirals. I'll autograph it with a personal message.
   (509-682-2383 or spiralsofjoy.com)
   Available as paperback or Kindle at Amazon.com.

3. Share your thoughts on your Facebook page.

4. Make comments on my Facebook pages: Go To Spirit with Jeanne McElvaney or Jeanne McElvaney.

5. Suggest it for a book club read.

6. Suggest it as a group read for friends, and then get together for coffee, cookies, and conversation using the Pondering Pages.

7. Review on Amazon.

8. Let me know! I love hearing from readers: jeanne@gotospirit.com

9. Continue your energy adventure. I'll be sharing *new* Ingredients, Energy Dialogues, and Guided Energies. Send me your email address to be part of the inner circle receiving new information: jeanne@gotospirit.com

10. Let me know about any group (10 or more) that could benefit from this book so I can give the participants a 10% discount.

11. Follow Guided Energies on YouTube and comment:
    (YouTube / Jeanne McElvaney)

Let's Connect!

Would you like to know more about me, my energy work, and my books? Maybe read my blogs?
GoToSpirit.com

Would you like to get Facebook energy posts and share your reading experience?
Go To Spirit with Jeanne McElvaney

Would you like to get supportive, insightful Facebook posts about childhood abuse and share your reading experience?
Jeanne McElvaney

Would you like to order this book or download to your Kindle?
Amazon

Would You like to have an autographed copy with a personal message?
spiralsofjoy.com or 509-682-2383

Would you like to listen to videos?
YouTube / Jeanne McElvaney

Would you like to read on-going articles about empowering yourself with energy?
GoLakeChelan.com/Evolve

Would you like to bring a group together for an energy event that we create especially for you?
Call Spirals in Chelan, WA   509-682-2383

Would you like a personal energy session
spiralsofjoy.com/classes-events-services/Jeanne McElvaney

Would you like to send me an email?
jeanne@gotospirit.com

Pondering Pages

While many of you will let the ingredients of change float through your feelings and thoughts, some of you might like to explore the ingredients with questions. Both are perfect. Igniting changes using energy is a very personal experience and trusting your journey is part of the adventure.

These questions can be journaling topics. They can be a guide if you choose to explore the ingredients with a group. They can be book club discussion-starters.

1. Do you celebrate the unique journey of others or want them to understand and follow your suggestions?

2. When you face difficult challenges, do you usually resist them and try to fix them, or do you see them as essential parts of your journey?

3. Who or what do you worry about? Do you have empowering thoughts that could reduce worry? Can you share some of those thoughts?

4. What are you doing to activate personal empowerment and growth?

5. In what ways are you an honorable witness to those you love, including yourself?

6. What reality shifts can you remember experiencing? Are you in the midst of a reality shift right now?

7. When you recognize a personal truth, how does it feel in your body?

8. Can you describe a few personal truths that you have been able to untangle from the truths of others?

9. Where is your focus currently centered?

10. Describe your future self or have a dialogue with her/him.

11. When you breathe deeply and shut down internal chatter, what energy insights come to you? Describe those insights.

12. What are some limiting emotions that swirl around you?

13. What persistent emotions would you like to release?

14. What outdated beliefs or expectations have you released?

15. What shifts in emotions has altered your beliefs in the past?

16. Being honest with yourself and noticing ambiguity, which relationships in your life are no longer working as you once thought they were?

17. Looking at your relationships with food, health, money, people, places and events, what do you want to change?

18. What experiences have "tickled" you, making you want "more please"?

19. Make a short list of magical words that reach the core of your being and describe what they make you feel.

20. Untangle old beliefs and connect to your inner child who still knows so much.

21. Looking back at your childhood and young adult days, what did you love to do and what did you dream of doing *someday*?

22. What new paths have you chosen to take as a result of inner nudges?

23. Seek your inner wisdom voice by emailing it as you would a trusted, caring friend. Let it *reply*.

24. Review life choices that required you to *leave the still pond of ease* so you could honor *your spirit's desire for more.*

25. Remember some times when worry, dread, or doubt blocked you from opportunities. Share them with your group or your journal.

26. Consider paths you've traveled that didn't serve your spirit; delve into the reasons you accepted those paths and why you stayed on them as long as you did.

27. List empowering insights you remember and, beside each one, list the actions you took as a result of the insight.

28. Remember times your emotional wounds were in charge and directing your choices. Are they still in charge??

29. Discuss or record the times when you felt so blocked you cried out "I've done everything I know how to do!" Name one way Quantum Thinking could have empowered your change.

30. Look at your life and see if you are getting lost in someone else's energy and, therefore, blocking your personal journey of change.

31. Alone or in a group, describe "Quantum Change" and "Quantum Loop".

What is the most significant thing you will take from this book?

Becoming an Author and Energy Healer

It all started sitting on a paint can. Taking a break from our project, my friend said, "You need to share this with people." We laughed when I asked what "this" was. The answer came out of one of those electric conversations when time disappears; she wanted me to share my life's journey of expanding personal possibilities.

Actually, it didn't _really_ start in that moment. Many years earlier, I had a life-changing shift while walking in a park with a friend who pointed to the leaves on a tree and told me they were vibrating molecules of energy. His remark opened the door to my understanding that everything was intelligent, communicating energy.

While the seed was planted that day, the fertile soil of looking past the usual was nurtured in rambling, wondering, exploring conversations with my mother during my teen years.

My passion to find ways to use the empowering insights from the quantum field blossomed while healing from childhood sexual abuse that had been dissociated until my early forties. We often find our superpowers when we face dragons of past wounds.

Along the way, family and friends contributed, encouraged, and celebrated. They shared their hearts, open minds, and fresh perceptions as I learned to translate the magic and complexities of Quantum Thinking into practical tools for change. Together we honed richly enlightening, exhilarating, deeply profound and fun ways to have conversations with the energy field.

Though it was my nature to stay small, the "paint can moment" kept nudging me to expand. How could I resist when I was seeing how harnessing energy could ignite the changes people craved? Personal and group sessions evolved. Writing books flowed into my desire to share the ways we can grow our lives with ease and joy.

Just like you, I have unmet desires, wishes, and challenges. The difference may be that studying energy has taught me that life doesn't happen to me; I'm creating my experience. Each time I recognize something I want to change, I *know* I get to use the ingredients in this book to bring it into my life. Like you, I'll be challenged to examine beliefs that keep me from moving forward. I'll have to work with my feelings and thoughts. And I'll be encouraged by Quantum Thinking as I explore what fits me best to ignite change. Over and over, I've seen that the balloons, rainbows, and ice cream cones of life are ours to have.

As a friend said, "I get it now. Quantum Thinking is not so much about making Old Thinking bad... as it is adapting to a new way of thinking."

More Reading Adventures With Jeanne

Old Maggie's Spirit Whispers

You have the answers. This tale reminds you to listen.

"What a delightful book. I will read this one more than once." Shannon F.

"Your books are magic." Janet F.

"When I read this book, I feel like I'm wrapping myself in a nice warm, fuzzy blanket... and than I realize that the blanket is me." BeverLi

"It's making me laugh out loud and brings tears to my eyes just as quickly. The grace and wisdom is wonderful." Roberta G.

Time Slipping

If you've ever imagined a personal retreat to explore your own possibilities, this novel is for you.

"Thank you for opening the door to spirit and letting it flood in. I have only read the first 30 pages and I'm hooked." Chevy K.

I just began reading this morning and I thought I was going to need to take a day off work to continue the journey. I am transported to another time when I slip into your books... you have an amazing way of creating presence." BeverLi

"**Time Slipping** will take you to the quiet place inside that knows exactly who you are, what you want, and how to find the courage to go for it." Morgan F.

Personal Development Insights

If you want a guide that reminds you energy holds uncommon answers and insights ~

"It's a shock to know that I get to choose my experience by choosing my thoughts and beliefs! It's quite miraculous." Marguerite D., "Personal Development Insights" Editor

"I will have to read it again and take notes." Gabriela of Quantum Heart Language

"You are a bright light on this planet." Barry S.

Spirit Unbroken: Abby's Story

~ 5-Star review and finalist in Readers Favorite Awards ~

A stunning novel of resilient spirit as childhood innocence is celebrated and violated. A nostalgic journey into 1950's small-town USA that takes the reader to the very core of dissociated memories.

"The wonder of this book is not in just showing the reader how it happens: Jeanne McElvaney has a wealth of research woven through the story as well as personal experience. It's a resource for survivors of abuse and PTSD as much as it is a novel." Sandra Bacon, Therapist

"Intense, honest, lyrical, funny, compelling, and incredibly well told. You reach the end better informed and wishing you could spend more time with the main character, Abby." Chevy K

"I am fascinated, mesmerized, horrified, and grateful to you. Your writing pulls me right into the story and childhood moments long forgotten." Pamela B.

Harrietta's Happenstance

A sweet, Jane Austen kind of romance floating on the surface of serious sexual abuse issues.

"I haven't been able to put it down... what a story... what characters." Darlene J.

"Your characters are wonderful, warm, and oh so inviting. I was there sharing their times no matter where they were." Cindy H.

"I love your book. The characters are real, the time period comes alive." Maura D.

Healing Insights

Empowering, positive guide for survivors ~

"You have such a powerful voice, full of grace, dignity, warmth, and understanding." Dr. Bob

"You have a special way of explaining in simple ways." Doris G.

"You have an uncanny ability to help people see more clearly what is happening to them." Suzan K

Childhood Abuse

A guide of empowering, gentle choices for change ~

"Your writing is so powerful. I marvel at how you figured all this stuff out!" Kathy L.

"Every chapter contained possibilities for joyous change. It answered questions I had been researching for years. It set down action steps." Mary L.

"Expressing gratitude and appreciation for sharing your messages of encouragement, empowerment and inspiration." Don P.

Amazon.com

Spirals
Ask to have a personal message and autograph.
509-682-2383 / spiralsofjoy.com

Alice: "This is impossible."

Mad Hatter: "Only if you believe it is."

"Alice in Wonderland"

by Lewis Carroll

Made in the USA
San Bernardino, CA
26 December 2017